CU00701339

MACEDONIA

THRACE

THASOS

SAMOTHRACE

GREECE

AEGEAN
SEA

ASIA
MINOR

THESSALY

Larisa

• Sardis

Delphi

BOEOTIA

Oropos

Athens

Ephesus

• Magnesia on the
Maeander

SAMOS

Perachora

Corinth

Isthmia

Mycenae

Argos

KEOS

PELOPONNESUS

Epidaurus

Nauplion

DELOS

NAXOS

Sparta

RHENIA

KOS

Knidos

Rhodes

MELOS

RHODES

Lindos

RANEAN
A

SEA OF CRETE

Kavousi

Isopata & Fortetsa

Mallia

Mochlos

Palaikastro

CRETE

Zakros

Idaean Cave

Hagia Triada

Inatos

Pyrgos

Myrtou

Metzolati Tou

Christos

Kofina Monofatsiou

Ship and Boat Models
in Ancient Greece

Ship and Boat Models
in Ancient Greece

BY PAUL FORSYTHE JOHNSTON

Naval Institute Press
Annapolis, Maryland

Copyright © 1985
by the United States Naval Institute
Annapolis, Maryland

Library of Congress Cataloging in Publication Data

Johnston, Paul Forsythe, 1950–
  Ship and boat models in ancient Greece.

  Bibliography: p.
  Includes index.
  1. Navigation—Greece.   2. Ship models—Catalogs.
3. Greece—Antiquities.   4. Near East—Antiquities.
5. Mediterranean Region—Antiquities.   I. Title.
VK75.J64   1985   623.8′21′0938   85–42759
ISBN 0–87021–628–7

Printed in the United States of America

To my parents

Contents

Illustrations

Acknowledgments

A large number of people and institutions provided invaluable assistance in preparing this study, and it is a pleasure to acknowledge that aid and its sources.

The book represents a revised and updated version of my doctoral dissertation, written for the Classical Archaeology Graduate Group at the University of Pennsylvania. Keith DeVries and Gregory Warden of the University of Pennsylvania and George Bass of the Institute of Nautical Archaeology and Texas A&M University formed my supervisory committee. G. Roger Edwards and Donald White, also of the University of Pennsylvania, were kind enough to direct my attention to some of the more obscure models in this corpus and supply photographs of others. The encouragement and thoughtfulness of these individuals were much appreciated.

Many others assisted by finding and passing along catalog entries gleaned from their own research, by photographing and measuring models in museums around the world that I was unable to visit, and by discussing various chronological, stylistic, and architectural criteria. I am especially grateful to John S. Morrison, J. Richard Steffy, Henry S. Robinson, Sharon Gibbs, Corethia Qualls, Polly Muhly, Alan Brooks, Cynthia Eiseman, Rhys and Helen Townsend, Nicholas Hartmann, Murray McClellan, Pamela Russell, Leslie Mechem, Anne Meulengracht-Madsen, William Murray, Leslie Simon, and Philip Young.

Most of the drawings for this study were prepared by Frederick and Caroline Hemans and by Vincent Amato. The text was edited and prepared for publication by Naval Institute Press editors Richard Hobbs and Linda LaMacchia. These people all worked to close deadlines with difficult materials, and their kindness and consideration are gratefully acknowledged.

I am particularly indebted to Arvid Göttlicher, whose *Materialien für ein Corpus der Schiffsmodelle im Altertum* was most helpful throughout the course of my research. Dr. Göttlicher also provided newly found models and offprints of his many articles on the subject, and I thank him for his generous aid and cooperation.

My last and greatest debt of gratitude is to my parents, without whose patience and unwavering support this study would not have been possible. It is to them that this book is dedicated.

Ship and Boat Models
in Ancient Greece

1

Introduction

Ancient Greek ship and boat models are unique among the various forms of evidence for ancient seafaring. They provide information totally lacking in two-dimensional representations of watercraft (wall and vase paintings), in low reliefs (coins, gems, seals, and relief sculpture), or in nautical archaeology (shipwrecks). In the first two categories, the artist or craftsman is limited in the accurate rendering of watercraft by the size, shape, and material of his medium. In nautical archaeology, the poor state of preservation of most ancient vessels limits the investigator's success. When a shipwreck is more than a few hundred years old, the remains are seldom preserved above the waterline, and details above the waterline must be hypothetically reconstructed or projected from exceedingly scanty evidence. However, at least in theory, a model builder is restricted only by his own ability to render a likeness of his subject matter; the relative overall proportions, the architectural details, and other related aspects may be precisely delineated. In practice, of course, it is usually impossible to determine exactly how accurately the craftsman has portrayed his subject. This problem is greatest for the most ancient models, for which so little comparative material survives that frequently their veracity cannot be judged.

For the purposes of this study, a model may be defined as a three-dimensional representation of a ship or boat, or its constituent elements. Thus, for example, a model in the round of a watercraft and a model of the prow or stern of a vessel receive equal treatment. The definitions used here for ships and boats are perhaps less dogmatic than those used by other modern scholars: a boat may be defined as a small watercraft (or small craft) generally intended for passage along local coastal or inland waterways and manned by a small crew. A ship may be defined as a large boat capable of and generally intended for (although not limited to) passage across open water. The crew of a ship may or may not be larger than that of a boat. Characteristics shared by both sorts of craft include the means of propulsion, which may be by pole, oar, paddle, or sail. The differences between a ship and a boat are for the most part arbitrary and modern; the distinction would probably never have been made in antiquity.

This study investigates ancient Greek ship and boat models made between the beginning of the Bronze Age and the end of the Hellenistic period (ca. 3000–31 B.C.). During the same years, however, other cultures around the Mediterranean and inland from its littorals also produced ship and boat models. During the Bronze Age in particular, Mesopotamia, Egypt, and Cyprus were major production centers. The Mesopotamian watercraft tradition, which includes both the earliest known representations of boats and the earliest known boat model (ca. 5000 B.C.),[1] comprises primarily small craft, often double-ended, with upturned ends and broad, beamy proportions. As might be expected, Mesopotamian models depict rivercraft rather than open water vessels. Like Greek models, Mesopotamian models are found in sacred, funerary, and to a lesser extent, domestic contexts throughout their period of production, which lasted at least into the Parthian period in the third century A.C.[2]

Boat models in Egypt are known from as long ago as the early Predynastic period, although the majority of models date from the time of the Great Pyramids (ca. 2770–1304 B.C.).[3] The earlier Predynastic models are rather amorphous and nonstandardized in their architecture, although most are flat-bottomed with high, rounded terminals.[4] During the later Bronze Age, the models are more normally papyriform in profile and represent small rivercraft propelled by pole, paddle, oar, and sail. Nearly all of the Bronze Age Egyptian models served as burial offerings and were intended to transport the deceased to and in the afterlife.[5] After a long hiatus beginning in the Late Bronze Age, models again appear in Egypt in the late Hellenistic period, when they adopt the form of small papyriform cargo boats. Production of this model type, which appears primarily in graves in the area of the Fayum, lasts possibly as late as the second century A.C.[6]

Cyprus was also a production center for ship and boat models from the Late Bronze Age through the Archaic period. Although Cypriote models exhibit their own peculiar architectural and decorative characteristics, they lie within the Greek *koiné*. Many of the

Bronze Age Cypriote examples have pseudo- or proto-rams rather like their contemporary Greek counterparts.[7] During the Late Geometric period, Cyprus produced (at least) three pairs of iron firedogs in the form of warships, which are virtually indistinguishable from the contemporary Greek examples found at mainland Argos and at Kavousi on Crete.[8] During the Cypro-Archaic period, models of Greek-style warships, small craft, and merchant vessels were manufactured on Cyprus, primarily at Amathus, Myrina, and Nikosia.[9] Nearly all of the Cypriote models with specific provenience have been found in graves, in which they served as burial offerings. There is little evidence that Cypriote models were intended to serve the decedent in the afterlife, as were their Egyptian counterparts.[10]

One of the most prolific sources of boat models during the period under discussion was the island of Sardinia, off the western coast of Italy. There, from the eighth through the sixth centuries B.C., the local culture produced a large quantity of small bronze small craft models, flat along the bottom with upcurved rounded ends. These models are frequently decorated with deer or bull protomes at the bow, fenestrated railings often surmounted with other animals, and suspension rings on a bracket straddling the boat's midsection. The distinctive architecture and decoration of these models reflect a purely local tradition with no mainland Italic or Greek influence.[11] The findspots for the Sardinian models are poorly documented, but from the few examples for which specific proveniences are known, it may be inferred that they served as burial or votive offerings or common household articles, such as lamps.[12] Crude warship models, small craft models ostensibly derived from a local dugout tradition, and boat-shaped vases also have occasionally been found from the pre-Republican and Republican periods on the Italic mainland.[13]

The modern literature devoted to ancient watercraft models is scanty at best. G. A. Reisner was the first to devote a specialized study to the topic, in his seminal 1913 monograph on ancient Egyptian ship and boat models in the Cairo Museum.[14] Reisner's study, which divided the known models into their various ship types and illustrated almost every example, became obsolete within a decade, primarily because many more models were discovered in nearly every royal Egyptian tomb excavated after its publication. The topic of Egyptian models has been partially updated by A. Göttlicher and W. Werner, whose recent brief publication conforms in outline to Reisner's volume.[15] Most recently, Göttlicher has published a monograph on ship models in antiquity, which by his definition include both ancient models and modern ethnographic models.[16] Prior to the present work, no specialized study has been devoted to the topic of ancient Greek watercraft models. To date, most of the material on the subject is contained in the various excavation reports on the sites where the models have been found; in addition, some of the better-known examples are briefly discussed in the several general handbooks on ancient seafaring.[17]

Subject to certain limitations, this study is intended to fill the breach. One limitation concerns the subject matter, which is strictly confined to Greek models, of which some 130 examples have survived. Although contemporary models from other areas around the Mediterranean (as outlined above) are occasionally cited for comparative purposes, their characteristics and development are largely distinct from, and for the most part unrelated to, those of Greek models. Some similarities of details are, of course, inevitable; when these arise, they are noted either in the text, in the footnotes, or in the catalog entries.

The other major limitation concerns the means by which the models have been studied. Most have been examined only through photographs or drawings supplied either in the primary publications or by the museums in whose collections the models are housed. These representations normally depict a model from a single perspective— usually from one or occasionally both of the sides, rarely from above. The catalog entries here are based both upon these renderings as available and upon the descriptions in the primary publication(s). The nature of the representations, which are frequently of marginal quality, and of the verbal descriptions, which are often written by individuals unfamiliar with watercraft architecture and terminology, inevitably leads to inaccuracies. Although every effort has been made in this study to correct these deficiencies, in some cases they may only be noted and not rectified. In other cases, some photographs or drawings, particularly those made prior to modern reconstruction and restoration, are more helpful in determining certain details than more recent photographs or even a physical examination of the model would be.[18]

2

Bronze Age

EARLY BRONZE AGE

While evidence for seafaring in Greece and the Aegean dates to at least as far back as the Mesolithic period,[1] the earliest representational evidence for seafaring in this region dates to the Early Bronze Age.[2] Included in this evidence are eight watercraft models, all from the Aegean islands: four from Crete, three said to come from Naxos, and a single example, of unknown provenience, which is identical to the Naxos craft in form and material (BA 6, discussed in this section). As far as is known at present, no watercraft models were made on mainland Greece during the Early and Middle Bronze Ages.[3]

Architecture

The models from the Cyclades (BA 3–6) appear to represent a discrete boat type. BA 3, the only intact example, is formed of three flat strips of lead. The bottom is flat, comprising slightly more than half the boat's length. Both ends rise at an angle to the bottom. One end terminates in a flat transomlike fashion, higher than the sides of the boat and approximately perpendicular to the bottom. The other end is fashioned into a point from the two lateral strips; the joint between them extends upward beyond the sides and is separated from them. BA 4–6 resemble BA 3 in the flat bottom, angular ends, and long narrow proportions. The length-to-beam ratio for BA 3 is 12.2:1 and was probably similar for BA 4–6. This extreme ratio, combined with the manifestly low sides of all of the Cycladic models, seems to indicate that they represent vessels derived from the dugout type of watercraft. Moreover, the sharp angle between the sides and bottom may indicate that they are dugouts of the more evolutionarily advanced extended type, in which wash strakes are added to the sides of the vessel to increase the freeboard.[4] The extended dugout, which is considered an intermediary evolutionary step between the monozygous dugout and the planked boat,[5] would be far more seaworthy in the Aegean Sea, where the seas are high and rough throughout the year.

Evidence for the means of propulsion of the Cycladic longboat is ambiguous. Contemporary evidence, in the form of the diagonal incisions outboard of either side of the boats engraved on the Cycladic terracotta "frying pans," may be interpreted as either oars or paddles.[6] Nor is there any evidence that the Early Cycladic boats used sails; the earliest appearance of sails in the Aegean was in Middle Minoan Crete.[7]

BA 3–6 superficially resemble the Cycladic "frying pan" boats in the angularity of hull profile, the raised ends, and the low freeboard. However, between the terracotta "frying pans" and the lead models, there are significant differences, which may indicate that they depict boats of disparate sizes, if not disparate types. The chief

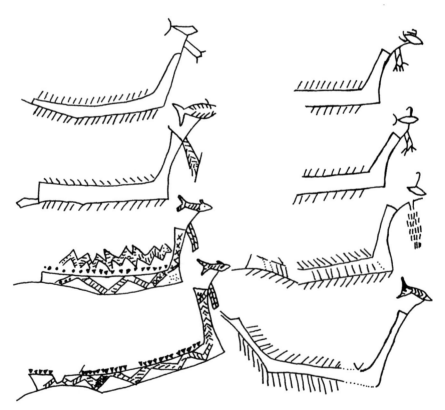

Early Cycladic "frying pan" longboats. After Gray, 1974: fig. 3.

difference is in the size and angles of the extremities of the boats: on the "frying pan" vessels, one end (always to the right side) is invariably much thicker, higher, and at a steeper angle to the bottom than the other. When preserved, this high end also invariably has a thin upwardly projecting engraved line with a tassel along its length and a fish at its peak. That both the fish and the tassel point away from the hull of the vessel has led many modern scholars to conclude that the high end to the right is the bow.[8] By contrast, on BA 3 both ends are of equal height and thickness[9] and are at an approximately equal angle to the flat bottom.[10] In addition, outboard of either hull side the "frying pan" craft incorporate between 12 and 26 diagonal engraved lines, which represent either oars or paddles, while the lead models have no decoration or embellishment beyond the hull itself.[11] Lastly, when preserved, the lower (left) ends of the "frying pan" craft have a projection emerging from and continuing the lower line of the hull. This projection, of uncertain purpose, may indicate the presence of a keel on the engraved longboats; this feature is clearly lacking on the flat-bottomed lead models. Taken together, these differences seem to indicate that boats of two disparate sizes, and possibly different types as well, are depicted by the lead models and the engraved Early Cycladic longboats.

The closest chronological and architectural analogy for the engraved Cycladic "frying pan" vessels comes not from the Cyclades, but from Palaikastro, Crete.[12] It is in the form of a clay boat model, BA 8. Points of concordance with the Cycladic longboats include the low profile, one high end and one low end, a steep angle between the high end and the bottom,[13] and a projection from the low end in the form of a spur.[14] However, BA 8 appears to depict a small craft rather than a large vessel, since its length-to-beam ratio is limited to 4.5:1.[15] Moreover, the presence of two thwarts or benches, which subdivide the boat's interior into three approximately equal compartments, indicates that a maximum of 2 rowers or paddlers could have been deployed along each side, as opposed to the 12–26 men per side for the Cycladic engraved longboats.[16] The rounded lower end and low freeboard further suggest that BA 8 is of the expanded dugout tradition.

The engraved longboats on the Early Cycladic "frying pans" and BA 8 are at the center of a modern controversy as to which end is the bow and which is the stern. Those advocating the high bow–low stern theory cite as evidence supporting their hypothesis the projection at the low end, which served as a "fixed rudder" at the stern to facilitate navigation in open water.[17] On the other hand, adherents to the low bow–high stern hypothesis interpret the projection as a ram,[18] as a debarkation point for the crew,[19] as a cutwater to permit better handling on the open sea,[20] or as an unexplained keel projection.[21] To these latter theories may be added the possibility that the spur served as an architectural prolongation of the keel to prevent damage from landings or groundings. Further, if the high thick end were the bow, it would be far heavier than the stern and thus lower in the water. Despite the pointed end, the extra weight would create more water resistance, causing the vessel to hog or dig into the sea, rather than to cut through or ride over the waves.[22]

Another factor favoring the high bow–low stern theory is cited by L. Cohen, who noted that BA 8 tapers toward the high end, which is pointed to cut the water.[23] However, primitive watercraft builders frequently designed their vessels with bows beamier than sterns, knowing empirically that the speed of a vessel through the water is affected more by turbulence at the stern than by the shape of the bow.[24] While rounded or bluff-bowed vessels are not in the majority among primitive watercraft, they are by no means uncommon.[25]

A third factor cited as evidence supporting the high bow–low stern premise involves the fish atop the high end of the "frying pan" longboats. The fish faces away from the hull of the vessel in every case. Proponents of the high bow–low stern theory consider this fish an ensign that, by analogy with a fish ensign on a Late Bronze Age ship painted on a pyxis from Pylos,[26] points in the direction in which the ship travels. They conclude that the high end of the Early Cycladic longboats and (by association) BA 8 must be the bow.[27]

Johnstone has made the strongest argument against this analogy by noting that recent reconstruction of the Pylos pyxis indicates that the animal ensign is a bird, not a fish.[28] His argument against the analogy may be strengthened by the observations that (1) the Pylos pyxis is of a much later date than the Early Bronze Age vessels; (2) the Pylos pyxis depicts a large decked sailing vessel from the Greek mainland, not an undecked man-propelled vessel in the dugout tradition from the Aegean islands; and (3) in the Late Bronze Age, ensigns could appear at either end of a vessel, not only at the bow.[29] Additionally, it may be argued that the "ensign" is a telltale or wind indicator, and not an ensign. In that or in any case, the fish might have pointed in either direction on the Cycladic longboats and was always depicted facing away from the hull by the gravers merely as an artistic convention to balance the composition. Convention and stylization are among the strongest impulses in Early Cycladic art.

Additional support for the low bow–high stern hypothesis may be found in the form of approximately contemporary ships from

Egypt.[30] As is the case in the Aegean during this period, most contemporary Bronze Age Egyptian watercraft are crude and ambiguous. However, a large group of Nubian rock cuttings, variously dated from the Predynastic to later periods,[31] show craft that are similar in profile to the Aegean vessels. With few exceptions, the rock cuttings that include steering oars on the vessels show them projecting from the higher end, an indication that this end must be the stern.[32] Similarly, two other Predynastic ship representations clearly show a steering oar at the higher end, a further indication that this end is the stern.[33]

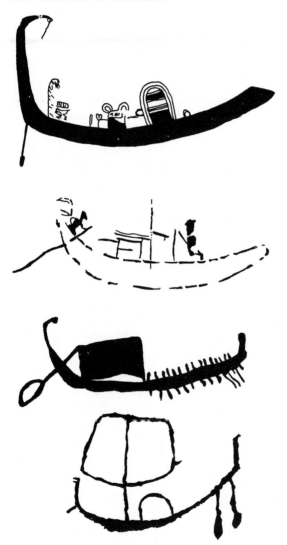

Predynastic Egyptian ships. Top after Bass, 1972:27, fig. 6; bottom three after Landström, 1970:figs. 22, 35, 39.

Supplementary evidence that Early Bronze Age longboats had low bows and high sterns is supplied by ethnographic analogy; that is, by comparing them to other primitive watercraft. The vessels of Polynesia, where navigation over open seas was commonplace, are particularly similar. These are normally expanded and extended dugouts, although they may also be planked vessels.[34] Like Egyptian watercraft, Polynesian watercraft usually incorporate a low bow and a high stern.[35] Many of these low-bowed, high-sterned vessels also include horizontal spurs at the bow, similar to those on BA 8 and the Early Cycladic "frying pan" longboats.[36] These spurs serve as bowsprits to which forestays are attached (on sail boats), as additional space for passengers or cargo, as gunwale extensions for more deck space, as platforms for tutelary deities, or as decoration. The points of attachment of these spurs show little uniformity; they may either extend directly from the keel or gunwale or extend from a point midway between.[37] It is perhaps significant in light of the analogy with Early Bronze Age Aegean vessels that all primitive Polynesian watercraft without exception are paddled, and not rowed.

By analogy, therefore, with both contemporary and ethnographic ships and representations,[38] it would seem that most of the evidence favors the theory that for the Cycladic longboats, the lead models, and their smaller Cretan counterparts, the low end with the projection is the bow, and the high, steeply angled end is the stern.

In general, the Cretan models from the Early Bronze Age are architecturally less uniform than their Cycladic equivalents. BA 1 and 2, from Mochlos, seem to offer evidence for a double-ended type of small craft. Bow and stern (if such a distinction may be made) on both of these flat-bottomed boats are identical: BA 1 has upswept ends almost half as high as the boat is long, and BA 2 is characterized by bifid projections at each end.[39] BA 2 also has two knobs vertically projecting above the gunwale from the interior; these knobs are variously interpreted as steering oars (?)[40] or as tholepins for oars.[41] If the latter interpretation is correct, BA 2 would prove conclusively that Early Minoan small craft were rowed, at least in some cases. However, other interpretations for these interior projections are possible. They might represent interior frames that extend above the gunwales for some unknown reason (rail stanchions?). Alternatively, they might depict either U-spreaders or stanchions to which outrigger booms could be attached, of a perishable material.[42] Outriggers are comparatively common upon primitive watercraft, although normally they are fastened flush to the gunwale rather than to stanchions.[43]

The closest parallels for these double-ended Early Minoan models come not from the Aegean or from Egypt, but from Mesopotamia, where water transport took place almost exclusively upon rivers. There, boat models and boat representations in other media from the end of the Ubaid period (ca. 3500 B.C.) onward almost invariably depict symmetrical double-ended small craft. The models from this period are all flat-bottomed, with vertical recurved or spiral terminals ending high above the gunwales, like those on BA 1. Vestigial keel projections are known to appear also on Mesopotamian boat models from the Neo-Sumerian period,[44] and upon a cylinder seal impression from Ur of the Early Dynastic I period.[45] During this early period, virtually all of the evidence for propulsion of Mesopotamian small craft indicates that they were paddled or punted, and not rowed.

Double-ended watercraft are also common among many primitive societies. They may adopt the form of simple dugouts, canoes with single or double outriggers, or double canoes.[46] Although in profile these craft are usually symmetrical, one end is nearly always designated as the bow and the other the stern by the position of steering equipment, masts, or thwarts. True double-ended vessels, for which the ends are completely interchangeable, are rare.[47] These vessels may also have one bifid end.[48] Double-ended craft with bifid ends like those on BA 2 are also recorded, but are rare.[49] Nearly all of these boats are small craft of the dugout type, perhaps an indication that BA 2 was similarly constructed. Having lasted from antiquity to the time of the modern whaling dory, symmetrical double-ended craft are some of the longest-lived and most widespread watercraft types in history.[50]

Functions

Except for BA 2, all of the Early Bronze Age Aegean boat models from excavation contexts are from burials.[51]

There are two theories concerning the use of boat models as burial offerings. The simpler of the two is that the model was a personal possession of the deceased and was considered valuable enough to be included among his burial offerings.[52] A corollary to this theory is that the deceased may have been a mariner, a profession that would account for the presence of a boat model, perhaps as a souvenir, among his possessions.[53] However, since at least one of the Early Bronze Age models was found in a domestic context, it cannot be said that boat models were manufactured exclusively as burial offerings during this period. This, in turn, raises the question of what purpose such an object might have served in daily life. At least for BA 2, there is no evidence that it was used as a lamp, since the excavation report makes no mention of any burning or deposit in the model's interior.[54] Other possibilities include use as a child's toy, a miniature objet d'art, a souvenir of maritime service, or a burial offering manufactured in the home but never used. In general, miniature objects in Early Bronze Age Greece and the Aegean are comparatively few in number and limited to only a few sorts of objects: anthropomorphic and theriomorphic figurines and vessels; jewelry and sealstones;[55] tools or ritual items such as double axes;[56] and boat, house, or shrine models.[57] Virtually all of these objects have been found in both domestic and funerary contexts, an indication that they were probably prized possessions in life as well as death.[58]

An alternative theory proposes a more metaphysical solution for the presence of boat models in graves: that they were manufactured and placed within the grave specifically to transport the decedent to or in the afterworld.[59] Although such a custom is well attested in Egyptian funerary practice from the Sixth Dynasty or possibly even earlier,[60] and perhaps in Mesopotamia as well from the Early Dynastic IIIA through the Neo-Sumerian periods,[61] there is no evidence for similar practices in Greece or the Aegean either in the Early Bronze Age or in any subsequent period.[62] The closest that the Greeks ever came to a concept of this sort was to tell of the ferryman Charon transporting the dead across the river Styx; however, this was a much later myth, judging from its first appearance in the seventh century B.C. *Minyad*.[63] During the Early Bronze Age, as C. Renfrew has stated, "Very few, if any, objects seem to have been made specifically for the grave . . . . There is no persuasive evidence for a belief in afterlife anywhere in the Aegean."[64]

MIDDLE BRONZE AGE

All four of the boat models attributed to the Middle Bronze Age are from Crete. As none have been published to date, it is not possible to discuss their architecture.

Functions

The Middle Bronze Age marks the earliest use of boat models in Greece, at least in Crete, as votive offerings at sanctuaries. The Middle Minoan period in general is characterized by the growth and spread of sanctuaries or cult places, many of which were caves or rock shelters originally used as dwellings.[65] At these and at urban sanctuaries, the miniature objects dedicated as votives greatly exceed in number and variety those placed in Early Bronze Age graves. They include realistic architectural models, furniture, terracotta triton shells, vases, and human body parts.[66] Miniature anthropomorphic and theriomorphic figurines, used in the Early Bronze Age as burial offerings, begin in the Middle Minoan period to appear as votives as well.[67]

Ship and boat models form only a tiny proportion of the votive simulacra of objects in everyday usage excavated to date from Middle Minoan sanctuaries. Miniature vases are by far the most common votive simulacra, where they appear at all.[68] On the basis of a unique representation of a woman seated in a boat upon a Late Minoan gold ring from Mochlos,[69] M. P. Nilsson has postulated the existence of a Minoan patron goddess of ships, seafaring, and navigation to whom (it may be presumed) votive boats would be dedicated.[70] Although, as Nilsson states, "There are . . . excellent reasons why the seafaring Minoans should have a goddess of navigation,"[71] there is no evidence for such a deity in the Middle Bronze Age,[72] since the Mochlos ring is later, and Middle Minoan boat votives appear at geographically dispersed and insecurely dated sites, as yet unpublished.[73] From this absence of evidence, it may be supposed that the boat models were dedicated by votaries about to embark upon a sea voyage, just returned from a successful voyage, or recently surviving a potentially hazardous voyage. In these cases, the offering would probably have been made to an individual's own patron deity, and not necessarily to a seafaring divinity.

At least one of the Middle Minoan models (BA 12) was found in a domestic context; two other Early-Middle Minoan transitional examples (BA 7 and 8) are from burials. These proveniences indicate continuity of function from the Early Bronze Age, from which models are known from similar contexts. Therefore, by the Middle Bronze Age, three primary applications for boat models have emerged: funerary, votive, and domestic. No additional applications are found in Greece or the Aegean until the Late Geometric period—a hiatus of approximately eight hundred years.[74]

LATE BRONZE AGE

Late Bronze Age ship and boat models are distributed over a far wider geographical area. Mainland Greece is included within the distribution pattern for the first time (BA 20–22, 25, 26). In addition, the Aegean islands (excluding Crete) contribute a larger proportion of examples than before: a total of five from Keos (BA 17, 18, 23) and Melos (BA 24 and 27). To date, only four Late Bronze Age models have been found from Crete: two from Hagia Triada (BA 14 and 15) and one each from Isopata (BA 16) and Mallia (BA 13). This pattern of movement away from Crete and toward the mainland

and islands may have been a minor manifestation of the overall cultural shift generated by the rapid growth and expansion of Mycenaean civilization during the Late Bronze Age; the Mycenaeans almost certainly derived the concept of fashioning boat models (and other objects) from the Minoans and possibly the Egyptians as well.

It is surprising, in light of the widespread distribution of Mycenaean trade goods throughout the Mediterranean and inland from its shores, that Mycenaean representational art includes comparatively few representations of ships and boats.[75] Furthermore, the majority of those depictions that are preserved appear to emulate Cretan paradigms, particularly in the glyptic arts.[76] The Linear B tablets, another potential source of information for Mycenaean seafaring, are equally unenlightening. The only significant document outlining nautical activity is a group of five tablets from Pylos that appear to list coast guard duty assignments for a body of some eight hundred men.[77] These men, responsible for guarding about 150 kilometers of coastline, seem to have belonged to eight different tribes. According to J. Chadwick, at least three-quarters of the tribal names are non-Greek, an indication that foreigners, not Mycenaeans, were employed as coastal watchers.[78] Moreover, since many of the same names appear among accounts of flax production,[79] one could conclude that coast guard duty was not of sufficient strategic importance to warrant full-time employment throughout the year. Another Pylos tablet mentions 30 men "going as rowers to Pleuron,"[80] yet no fewer than five hometowns are listed for the men. This suggests that seafaring was not a primary vocation for the region. Despite the defensive implications of employing a large body of men in the coast guard, the many palace accounts and inventories, which are replete with lists of a great variety of crafts, industries, and military paraphernalia, do not mention any shipbuilding industry or stockpiling of ships' parts.[81]

The relative dearth of nautically inspired Mycenaean art before the end of the Late Helladic IIIB period,[82] combined with the evidence of the Linear B tablets on the subject of seafaring, tends to challenge the traditional view advocating a Mycenaean thalassocracy.[83]

Only one boat model from the Late Bronze Age is positively dated to the first phase (BA 13, dated to the Late Minoan IA period), and only one is attributed tentatively by its excavator to the second phase (BA 17, dated to the Late Minoan IB/Late Helladic II period or earlier).[84] The remainder are dated with uncertainty either to the third phase (Late Minoan or Helladic III) or to the Late Bronze Age in general.

Architecture

By the Late Bronze Age, sailing ships are depicted in various media (wall and vase paintings, seals and their impressions, etc.) more frequently than are other ship or boat types. However, the opposite is true for models of ships and boats: only one example (BA 15) may be identified with certainty as a sailing vessel. It has the form of a beamy cargo vessel (having a restored length-to-beam ratio of 3.2:1) with a flattened bottom, steeply sheered sides, and nearly perpendicular stem- and sternposts. Just below gunwale level is a deck that covers approximately three-quarters of the hull's interior; the remainder is taken up by two hatches, one at either end of the vessel, which provide access to the hold. A thick mast stub rises vertically from the bottom of the hold through the deck, but is broken off just above deck level. That it is set closer to one end of the vessel indicates that that end is the bow. The larger of the two hatches is at the stern and covers the entire space between opposite gunwales. The smaller oblong bow hatch does not extend to the gunwales, but is centered in the middle of the deck. A wide thwart with two badly worn excrescences of uncertain purpose is preserved aft of the mast stub, 1.5 centimeters above deck level.[85] Forward of the mast are the remains of another smaller thwart on either side of the hull. Together the thwarts may represent benches,[86] or possibly mast partners. In addition, there is a projection at one end that may depict the tiller of a steering oar.[87]

In incorporating decks high in the hull structure,[88] BA 15, from Hagia Triada, closely resembles two merchant vessels illustrated upon a Late Helladic IIIB:1 krater from Enkomi, Cyprus.[89] In addition, stem- and sternposts on both BA 15 and the Enkomi boats are almost perpendicular to the flat bottom. The Enkomi craft also incorporate at one end a below-decks bulkhead that subdivides the hold into two unequal compartments and may also serve as a deck stanchion or hatch support. From their comparative hold depths, it may be inferred that BA 15 and the Enkomi vessels represent roomy merchantmen with deep cargo holds and overhead decks covering most of the ships' lengths. Unfortunately, the date of BA 15 is disputed; if it is from the Late Minoan I or II period,[90] it is the earliest evidence in the Mediterranean for decked ships.[91] The other boat model from Hagia Triada (BA 14) is of little architectural interest.

BA 23 and BA 25 appear to represent large galleys, which may or may not have had auxiliary sail power.[92] Both have long, low proportions, although the length-to-beam ratio cannot be determined for either on account of their fragmentary condition. BA 23 is the broader of the two, with a steeply upswept sternpost, an indentation along the hull's interior which may delineate the keel, and steep sides which meet the bottom at a sharp angle at or near the waterline. BA 25, of which only the bow and stern are preserved, has a high stem-post merging into an oversized bow compartment at the top and a low, horizontally projecting forefoot. The sternpost also is exaggeratedly thick and large and rises steeply from the flat bottom. In the afterbody is a raised thwart, which probably served as an axle housing for wheels used to move the model along the ground.[93] Two additional holes running thwartships through the top and base of the bow compartment probably held a string halter for pulling the model, although the upper hole may have served as an anchor point for a forestay.[94] Similar holes appear on the preserved forefoot of BA 18, although here they are horizontally oriented, rather than vertically as they are on BA 25.

By the Late Bronze Age, the projecting forefoot is a common feature on many of the extant ship representations.[95] It first appears in the Aegean upon the earliest ships from that region, the Early Cycladic "frying pan" longboats. The same feature appears contemporaneously in Crete,[96] and later among the earliest ship representations from the mainland.[97] In the Bronze Age, there is no evidence that this projection served as an offensive ram, since in representations it never projects far enough forward to prevent the ramming vessel from damaging itself as well as the vessel being rammed.[98] And although there is literary evidence for naval warfare in the Late Bronze Age,[99] it does not mention ramming as a tactic. Homer also is silent regarding naval tactics or conflicts, for both the period he described and the period in which he lived. Therefore, in the absence of any evidence to the contrary, it may be assumed that the forefoot served some nonmilitary function; for example, it may have been a cutwater, a bow bumper, a "primitive (architectural) survival," [100] or "the ancient way of handling the troublesome joint between stem and keel."[101] A similar construction found at the bow of a fourth century B.C. shipwreck is considered by some to be an offensive ram, although this interpretation is debatable.[102]

The remaining Late Bronze Age models appear to represent small craft, not the larger seagoing vessels that are more normally depicted in other media. Thus, like the earlier models BA 8 and BA 12, BA 20 has two interior thwarts, indicating that the artist probably intended a likeness of a small craft with two benches. In profile, BA 20 closely resembles three of the small craft manned by one or two men depicted on the Miniature Fresco from Thera, which dates to the Late Minoan IA period.[103] The fresco boats and BA 20 share gently curved terminals and low hulls; however, unlike BA 20, the

Late Minoan IA small craft from Theran Miniature Fresco. After Marinatos, 1974:colorplate 9.

fresco small craft have marginally more slender bows than sterns, much like smaller versions of the large vessels they accompany. That all but one of the Miniature Fresco ships and boats are propelled by men with paddles rather than oars may indicate a similar means of propulsion for BA 20.[104]

BA 19 also is identifiable as a small craft by the small number of frames painted on the interior. Like BA 20, BA 19 is broad amidships and tapers sharply to a point at either end. The bow is marked on each side by an oculus. This is the earliest appearance in the Mediterranean of this feature, antedating the next occurrence by several hundred years.[105] The bow is also endowed with a high, strongly articulated stempost, slightly sheered, which extends aft for one-sixth of the boat's length before joining the hull's basal line (keel?) at an obtuse angle. Unlike the frames on BA 26, those on BA 19 are painted on both the interior and exterior of the hull. The gunwale or rail is formed by a wavy line along its upper surface, and the ribs meet the rail at the crests of the wavy lines, so that the hull appears to sag slightly between the frames. This unusual feature has led some scholars to speculate that BA 19 depicts a skin shell over a wooden framework.[106] This theory may be strengthened by the fact that under certain circumstances the hide hull of a skin boat is transparent, so that the interior framework may be seen from the outside, as it may on BA 19.[107] However, a primary characteristic of skin boats is light, closely set framing, since the framework supplies all of the lateral and longitudinal strength of the vessel.[108] Such does not appear to be the case for BA 19, on which the frames are as heavy and as distantly spaced as they are on BA 26, which must be nearly the same size and is indisputably a planked boat.

Functions

As was mentioned earlier, no new functions for ship and boat models appear during the Late Bronze Age, at least for those models with known proveniences. Thus, of this group, which totals 11 examples, 4 are from domestic contexts (BA 13, 14, 19, and 22) and 5 served as votives (BA 15, 17, 18, 21, and 23). Two more examples were used as burial offerings (BA 16 and 20), a use indicating continuity of function from the Early Bronze Age. Although models from funerary contexts are not yet documented from the Middle Bronze Age, there is too little evidence from this period to be certain that models were not used as burial offerings then as well.

CATALOG

Catalog entries are arranged chronologically, as far as possible. Dates are those assigned by the original excavator, unless otherwise indicated. Disputed dates are followed by their proponent(s). Bibliographical citations are limited to the major sources for a particular entry; purely descriptive references or those that only mention an entry in passing are omitted. Entries are as complete as possible, given the available information. Primary publications of an object are marked by an asterisk (*) preceding the author's name.

BA 1. Boat model from cemetery of Mochlos, found in loose soil.
Early Minoan I or II
Burial offering
Length (L): 19 cm; Height (H): 9 cm
Heraklion, Heraklion Museum (?)

Evans, 1921–35 (vol. 1):57, fig. 16c; Gray, 1974:G15, no. A14; Nilsson, 1950:188–89, fig. 88; *Seager, 1912:82, 93, fig. 48, no. 31.

Coarse, red-clay model of small craft, intact. Flat bottom, with identical ends rising almost vertically from bottom. Terminals are rounded, ending high above gunwale.

BA 2. Boat model from house deposit, Block A, Mochlos.
Early Minoan I or II
Domestic context
L: 20 cm; beam (B): 3.5 cm; L:B ratio 5.6:1
Heraklion, Heraklion Museum 5570

Basch, 1975:201, fig. 1; Bass, 1972:17, pl. 14; Behn, 1927/28:241, pl. 61.1; Bonino, 1975:15–17, fig. 5A; Casson, 1971:34–35, fig. 54; Cohen, 1938:486–89, fig. 2; Göttlicher, 1978:61, no. 313, pl. 24; Gray, 1974:G15, no. A14; Hutchinson, 1962:91–92, fig. 13; Laviosa, 1969–70:17, 19; Marinatos, 1933:173, no. 20, pp. 174, 215, 217, pl. 14.20; *Seager, 1909:279, fig. 2, p. 290; Zervos, 1956:10, 37, 41, pl. 141.

BA 2. Drawing by Vincent Amato, after Göttlicher, 1978.

Intact clay model of small craft. Flat bottom, with identical bifid ends. Lower bifid projection at both ends extends nearly horizontally from boat bottom. Four interior knobs or spurs, set in two pairs against opposite gunwales, project high above sides of boat.

BA 3. Boat model from cist grave, Naxos (?).
Early Cycladic
Burial offering
L: 40.3 cm; B: 3.3 cm; L:B ratio: 12.2:1
Oxford, Ashmolean Museum 1929.26

Bass, 1972:17, 29, fig. 13; Buchholz, 1972:27, no. 25, fig. 7; Buchholz and Karageorghis, 1970:86, no. 1076; Casson, 1971:41; Doumas, 1968:285–86; Göttlicher, 1978:63, no. 328, pl. 25; Gray, 1974:G14, no. A2, G34, n. 50a; Hood, 1971:126, 231, pl. 107; Humphreys, 1973:219; Johnstone, 1973:8–10, fig. 8; Laviosa, 1969–70:16, 26, n. 2; *Renfrew, 1967:5, 17–18, no. 12, pls. 1, 3; Renfrew, 1972:356–58, fig. 17.7, pl. 28.4.

Intact flat-bottomed boat model crafted of three flat strips of Siphnian lead joined at the basal surface. Long, slender proportions. Bow and stern of approximately equal height. Strongly sheered and

BA 3. Courtesy of the Ashmolean Museum, Oxford, England.

BA 4. Courtesy of the Ashmolean Museum, Oxford.

pointed bow meets bottom at steep angle. Canted stern meets bottom
at shallower angle than bow and is finished in a transomlike flat strip,
formed by a 90-degree fold of the bottom strip.

BA 4. Boat model from cist grave, Naxos (?).
Early Cycladic
Burial offering
Preserved L: 34 cm
Oxford, Ashmolean Museum 1938.726

Buchholz, 1972:27, no. 25; Casson, 1971:41; Doumas, 1968:285–86;
Göttlicher, 1978:63, no. 330, pl. 25; Gray, 1974:G34, no. A2; Humphreys, 1973:219; Johnstone, 1973:8–10, fig. 8; Laviosa, 1969–70:16,
26, n. 2; *Renfrew, 1967:5, 17–18, no. 14; 1972: 356–58, pl. 28.

Fragmentary lead boat, in two pieces. Portion of hull amidships
missing. Similar to BA 3.

BA 5. Boat model from cist grave, Naxos (?).
Early Cycladic
Burial offering
Preserved L: 39 cm
Oxford, Ashmolean Museum 1938.725

BA 5. Courtesy of the Ashmolean Museum, Oxford.

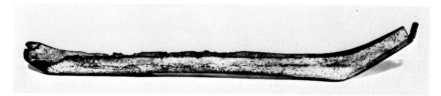

BA 6, port side. Courtesy of the Merseyside County Museums, Liverpool, England.

Buchholz, 1972:27, no. 25; Casson, 1971:41; Doumas, 1968:285–86; Göttlicher, 1978:63, no. 329, pl. 25; Gray, 1974:G14, no. A2; Humphreys, 1973:219; Johnstone, 1973:8–10, fig. 8; Laviosa, 1969–70:16, 26, n. 2; *Renfrew, 1967:5, 17–18, no. 13, pl. 3; 1972:356–58, pl. 28.3.

Fragmentary lead boat, in two pieces. Stern and hull section missing. Originally the largest of the Naxos lead boats. Similar to BA 3 and 4.

BA 6. Boat model from cist grave, Naxos (?).
Early Cycladic
Burial offering
Preserved L: 38 cm
Liverpool, Merseyside County Museum 55.66.180 (formerly collection of R. G. Bosanquet)
*Göttlicher, 1978:63, no. 330a, whence *Kunst und Kultur der Kykladen* (Ausst.-Kat. Karlsruhe, 1976), no. 457, with figures.

Fragmentary lead boat, like BA 3–5. Portion of stern missing. Flat bottom slightly convex (or hogged) in profile. Probably the fourth of four lead boats said to come from Naxos cist grave, of which BA 3–5 are the other three.[109]

BA 7. Boat model from Tholos X, Christos, Mesara Plain, Crete.
Early Minoan III–Middle Minoan I
Burial offering
L: 9.5 cm; B: 2.5 cm; L:B ratio: 3.8:1
Heraklion, Heraklion Museum

Göttlicher, 1978:61, no. 315, pl. 24; Gray, 1974:G15, no. A(15); Marinatos, 1933:174, no. 21, 180, 184, fig. 1b, 217, pl. XIV.21; *Xanthoudides, 1924:72, pl. XLb.

BA 7. Drawing by the author, after Marinatos, 1933.

Limestone boat model, partially restored.[110] Pointed bow and rounded stern are of equal height. On interior, elevated section sloping aft and covering forward third of hull may represent a foredeck.

BA 8. Boat model from burial enclosure ossuary, Palaikastro.
Early–Middle Minoan (*Dawkins)
Early Minoan II (Marinatos)
Burial offering
L: 19.5 cm; B: 4.3 cm; L:B ratio: 4.5:1
Heraklion, Heraklion Museum, Vitrine 10, lowest shelf

Basch, 1975:201; Bass, 1972:17, fig. 12; Behn, 1927/28:240, pl. 61b; Betts, 1973:326; Bosanquet and Dawkins, 1923:7, figs. 3k and 4; Casson, 1971:34–35, 41, fig. 23; 1975:3, 9, 10, n. 17; Cohen, 1938:489–90, fig. 4; *Dawkins, 1903–4:196–98, fig. 1k; Göttlicher, 1978:61, no. 314, pl. 24; Gray, 1974:G14, no. A1, G34, G40, G80, fig. 3k;

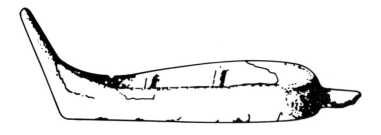

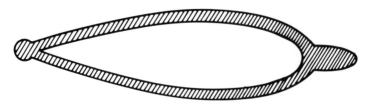

BA 8. Drawing by Vincent Amato, after Evans, 1926 (top) and Marinatos, 1933 (bottom).

Herbig, 1940:62, Hutchinson, 1962:92–93, fig. 14; Johnstone, 1973:6, 10, fig. 6; Köster, 1923:63, 86, pl. 15; Marinatos, 1933:173, no. 19, 180, 183–84, fig. 1a, 196, 212, 217, pls. XIII, XIV, no. 19; Stillwell, 1952:196.

Clay model of flat-bottomed small craft, restored at bow, along gunwale, and on bottom. Two thwarts connected to opposite sides just below gunwale level divide interior into three equal compartments and probably represent either benches or thwarts. Low, rounded bow has long, blunt forefoot projecting horizontally forward just above level of flat bottom. High, sharp stern is at 65-degree angle to bottom, resembling that of BA 3. In plan, boat is teardrop-shaped,[111] with greatest beam slightly forward of amidships.

BA 9. Boat model from peak sanctuary, Metzolati tou Kofina Monofatsiou, Crete.
Middle Minoan III (Long)
Votive
Dimensions unknown
Heraklion, Heraklion Museum 16437 (Case 21)

Unpublished. Mentioned by Faure, 1967:124–25; Göttlicher, 1978:62, no. 324; Laviosa, 1969–70:29, n. 3; Long, 1974:48, 52, n. 52.

Fragmentary clay boat; "part of a boat with benches and an upcurved prow found in the Middle Minoan III peak sanctuary."[112]

BA 10. Boat model from Pyrgos Myrtou, Crete.
Middle Minoan (Alexiou)
Function unknown
Dimensions unknown
Heraklion, Heraklion Museum (?)

Unpublished. Mentioned by Alexiou, 1976:205.

BA 11. Boat model from chasm east of sanctuary at Traostalos, Crete.
Middle Minoan (Alexiou)
Votive
Dimensions unknown
Heraklion, Heraklion Museum (?)

Unpublished. Mentioned by Alexiou, 1971:320; 1976:205.

BA 12. Boat model from outside east corner, Building H, Zakros, Crete.
Middle Minoan (Alexiou)
Domestic context
Dimensions unknown
Heraklion, Heraklion Museum 19444

Unpublished. Mentioned by Alexiou, 1976:205; Long, 1974:48, 52, n. 52; Orlandos, 1970–71:177; Sakellarakis, 1971:197.

"Part of the stern of a clay boat, with two benches (thwarts?) and a man turned toward the prow."[113] Upcurved stern.[114]

BA 13. Boat model from Room XVI, Maison de la Façade à Redans, Mallia, Crete.
Late Minoan IA
Domestic context
L: 3 cm; B: 2 cm
Heraklion, Heraklion Museum 17.159 (Λ123)

Unpublished. Mentioned by Van Effenterre, 1969:103.

"Red clay with brownish slip. Oblong form imitating a rudimentary boat."[115]

BA 14. Boat model from villa, Hagia Triada.[116]
Late Minoan I or II
Domestic context
Preserved L: 14 cm; B: 4.8 cm (inside)
Heraklion, Heraklion Museum 344 (Vitrine 143)

Göttlicher, 1978:62, no. 320, pl. 24; Gray, 1974:G18, no. C 31; Laviosa, 1969–70:21, fig. 16; Long 1974:48, 52, n. 53; Marinatos, 1933:174, no. 22, 215, 217, fig. lc, pl. XIV.22; *Anonymous, *RendLinc* 12 (1905): 334; Sakellarakis, 1971:199.

White marble or alabaster boat model,[117] restored on starboard side and at tip of bow. Sharply pointed bow is higher than rounded stern, as restored. Maximum beam is slightly forward of amidships. Rounded molding along upper surface represents either gunwale or cap rail. Hole at base of stern may indicate use of model as rhyton.[118]

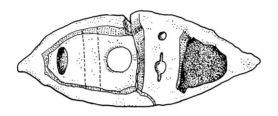

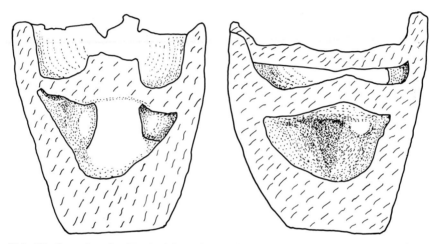

BA 15. Drawing by Frederick and Caroline Hemans, after Banti, 1941–
43 (plan) and Laviosa, 1972 (section).

BA 15. Boat model from Piazzale dei Sacelli, Hagia Triada, Crete.
Late Minoan I (Gray)
Late Minoan I–II (Marinatos)
Late Minoan II (Kirk)
Late Minoan III (Alexiou)
Late Minoan IIIC (Laviosa)
Votive (?)
Preserved L: 21.5 cm; B: 8 cm; H: 8.5 cm (Laviosa)
Preserved L: 23 cm; B: 7 cm (interior) (Marinatos)
L:B ratio: 3.2:1 (from restored photographs)
Heraklion, Heraklion Museum 3141

Alexiou, 1976:205; Banti, 1941–43:63, figs. 65a–b; Göttlicher, 1978:62,
no. 319; Gray, 1974:G18, no. C 32, G46, G83–84; Kirk, 1949:139,
n. 58; Laviosa, 1969–70:27, figs. 27a–d; Marinatos, 1933:174, no.
23, 195, 205, 216, fig. 5, pl. XIV.23; *Paribeni, 1908:26, n. 5.

Fragmentary clay model of flat-bottomed sailing vessel, in two pieces. Both ends, edge of one side, and forward thwart restored. Traces of red paint along inside of gunwale and on after thwart. In profile, bow and stern rise nearly vertically from bottom. Small hatch at bow and larger hatch at stern provide access to hold below. Mast stub preserved from bottom of interior through deck, ending below thwart level. Mast is closer to one end, an indication that it is the bow. After (preserved) thwart is wider than forward thwart and has on upper surface two badly abraded excrescences of uncertain purpose. Thwarts may represent either mast partners or benches; if the latter, the model depicts an oared sailing vessel. Preserved thwart is 1.5 centimeters above deck level; deck is 2.5 centimeters below gunwale or cap rail. Small projection at one end may represent tiller of steering oar.[119]

BA 16. Boat model from Isopata, Crete.

Late Minoan II (?)

Burial offering

Dimensions unknown

Heraklion, Heraklion Museum (?)

Unpublished. Mentioned by Göttlicher, 1978:62, no. 323; Schachermeyr, 1964:172.

Possibly ivory.[120]

BA 17. Boat model from −0.3 meters, Corridor 7, Temple, Agia Irini, Keos.

Late Minoan IA−B

Votive

Preserved L: 13.4 cm; preserved B: 4.8 cm

Athens, National Archaeological Museum K3.600

Caskey, 1964a:417, pl. 493b; *Caskey, 1964b:327, pl. 56c; Gray, 1974:G20, no. C 59, G53.

One end and part of hull of broad-bottomed bronze boat is preserved; remainder is missing. Tapering, pointed end curves upward gradually to a thin, high terminal. Hull bent where broken off. Longitudinal raised ridge along center line of hull's interior may represent keelson. Possibly associated with BA 23.

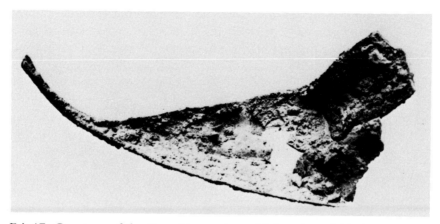

BA 17. Courtesy of the Keos Excavations, University of Cincinnati.

BA 18. Boat model from stone-lined pit or bothros A1 over Room XIII (domestic storeroom), Agia Irini, Keos.

Late Helladic IIIA.2–B.1

Votive (?)

Preserved L: 5.5 cm; preserved B: 3.4 cm; preserved H: 1.7 cm

Athens, National Archaeological Museum or Keos, Keos Museum K1.182

*Caskey, 1962:273, pl. 99f; Göttlicher, 1978:63, no. 331; Gray, 1974:G20, no. C 58, pl. 1d; Long, 1974:52, n. 51.

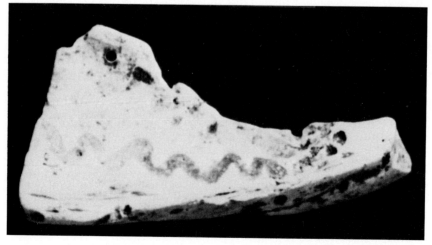

BA 18. Courtesy of the Keos Excavations, University of Cincinnati.

Fragmentary forefoot (?) of clay boat model, broken at both ends. Painted wavy line may represent waves. Two small holes are preserved; one at upper edge near base, the other at upper edge near tip of forefoot.

BA 19. Boat model from Room C5:1 or C5:8, Phylakopi, Melos.
Mycenaean
Domestic context
Preserved L: 12.7 cm; B: 3.6 cm; H: 1.8 cm
Athens, National Archaeological Museum 9892(707) or 9893

Bosanquet and Welch, in the work of Atkinson, 1904:11, 206, fig. 180; Cook, in the work of Whibley, 1931:568, fig. 123; Behn, 1927/28:241, pl. 61.2; Göttlicher, 1978:61, no. 317, pl. 24; Gray, 1974:G19, no. C 42, G51, G60, figs. 14a–b; Kirk, 1949:132–33; Köster, 1923:57, fig. 9; Laviosa, 1969–70:24, n. 3, fig. 22; Marinatos, 1933:175, no. 26, 180, 216–17, pl. XV.26; Morrison and Williams, 1968:11, BA 7, 82; *C. H. Smith, 1896–97:22–25, figs. 1–2; A. N. Stillwell, 1952:196.

Clay model of small craft, with minor portions of bow and stern missing. Decoration in white slip, with details (ribs, oculus, etc.) in black glaze. Details in black include seven frames, delineated on both interior and exterior, interior longitudinal bulkhead (?) at stern, and circular oculus with dot iris on either side of bow. In plan, gunwale or cap rail follows a wavy line; frames correspond to wave crests, with hull sagging inward between them. Sagging hull, combined with frames depicted inside and outside, may indicate that vessel is skin-hulled boat of frame-first construction. Stem, marked by presence of earliest oculus in the Aegean, consists of thick stempost meeting bottom of model at slight angle. Boat bottom is slightly rockered; cutaway stem has long overhang.

BA 19. Courtesy of the National Archaeological Museum, Athens, Greece.

BA 20. Courtesy of the National Archaeological Museum, Athens, Greece.

BA 20. Boat model from Chamber Tomb 79, Mycenae.
Late Helladic IIIB–C (Laviosa)
Burial offering
Preserved L: 7 cm; preserved H: 2 cm (Göttlicher)
Athens, National Archaeological Museum 3099

Cohen 1938:487; Göttlicher, 1978:64, no. 334, pl. 25; Gray, 1974: G19, no. C 44, G55; Laviosa, 1969–70:26–27, figs. 26a–b; Long, 1974:48, 52, n. 52, pl. 24, fig. 70; *Marinatos, 1933:174, no. 25, 180, 215, 217, pl. XIV.25.

Clay model of flat-bottomed small craft. One end (nearest thwarts) restored; other end lacking small splinters. Traces of black paint on interior, exterior, and on ends, where it "makes a sort of large disc on each side."[121] Point of widest beam is amidships, narrowing sharply to ends. Preserved end rises to point. Two interior thwarts (benches?), the larger curved and the smaller straight, are asymmetrically placed closer to the restored end.

BA 21. Boat model from Mycenaean fountain fill, Acropolis, Athens.
Late Helladic IIIC (?)
Votive
Preserved H: 11 cm
Athens, National Archaeological Museum AF 1066

*Broneer, 1939:408, fig. 89v; Göttlicher, 1978:64, no. 336; Gray, 1974:G20, no. C 57, G53, pl. 1c.

Fragmentary forefoot of model of large seagoing vessel, of dark red clay. In two pieces. Decoration in cream-colored matt paint.

BA 21. Courtesy of the American School of Classical Studies at Athens: Agora Excavations, Athens, Greece.

"The designs consist of horizontal and wavy lines, short independent cross lines, etc."[122] Traces of black-painted stripes on bottom of interior, longitudinally disposed. Hull originally flat-bottomed. Stempost slightly raked.

BA 22. Boat model from Citadel House Area, Mycenae.
Late Helladic IIIC
Domestic context
Preserved L: 7.1 cm; preserved H: 3.5 cm; H (of side): 2 cm
Nauplion, Nauplion Museum. Excavation no. 64-367
*Tamvaki, 1973:256, no. 259(64-367), fig. 24.259, pl. 52d.259.

Fragmentary clay boat model, comprising section of hull and one end. Tip of end missing. Decoration consists of "monochrome, rather metallic-looking paint both on the inside and outside."[123] On exterior, pronounced axial bulge along bottom represents keel and stempost or sternpost. End rises sharply from bottom, which appears to have originally been flat. In plan, end tapers strongly to point, possibly an indication that it is the bow.

BA 23. Boat model from Corridor VII, Temple, Agia Irini, Keos.
Late Minoan IB–Late Helladic IIA (Long)

BA 22. Drawing by Vincent Amato, after Tamvaki, 1973.

Votive

Dimensions unknown

Athens, National Archaeological Museum (Long)[124]

Keos, Keos Museum (Göttlicher)

Göttlicher, 1978:64, no. 335, pl. 25; Long, 1974:48, 52, n. 51, pl. 24, fig. 69.[125]

    Fragmentary bronze boat model; section of one end and hull preserved; remainder missing. Axial longitudinal depression visible on interior may represent keel. Sides meet bottom at steep angle. Preserved end curves upward sharply into point, of which tip is missing. Possibly associated with BA 17.

BA 24. Boat model from Phylakopi, Melos.

Mycenaean (Morrison and Williams)

Geometric (Göttlicher)

Findspot unknown

Preserved L: 6 cm; preserved H: 4.5 cm

Athens, National Archaeological Museum 9893

*Bosanquet and Welch, in the work of Atkinson, 1904:206–7, pl. 40, 37; Casson, 1971:35, n. 11; Cohen, 1938:487, n. 4; Göttlicher, 1978:62, no. 321, pl. 25; Gray, 1974:G19, no. C 43, G51; Laviosa, 1969–70:17–18, figs. 11a–b; Marinatos, 1933:175, no. 27, 215, pl. XV.27; Morrison and Williams, 1968:11, BA 6.

    Boat model of light buff clay. One fragmentary bifid end preserved; tip of lower projection missing. Preserved portion indicates that boat was originally flat-bottomed. Pale slip, flaking, covers preserved portion. Brown-painted strip delineates gunwale or cap rail on one side; strip is doubled on other side, offsetting gunwale from cap rail.

BA 24. Photograph by the author.

BA 25. Boat model from Oropos (?).
Middle–Late Helladic (Touchais)
Probably Late Helladic III (Iakovides)
Probably Mycenaean (Catling)
Geometric (Petrakos)
Function unknown
Restored L: ca. 35 cm; restored B: 8.3 cm
Present location unknown

Catling, 1979:7–8, fig. 5; S. Iakovides, personal communication, 1981; *Petrakos, 1974:98–99, pl. 57 α–γ; Touchais, 1978:655–56, fig. 35.

Pink clay model of flat-bottomed galley; heavily restored throughout. Bow section comprises high, slightly sheered stempost with transverse holes at top and bottom (diameter: 0.3 cm) above forefoot and vertical hole on uppermost surface of forefoot. Transverse holes probably for attaching line to drag model. Base of forefoot is above level of flat bottom and projects substantially beyond stempost. Forefoot may be ram. Stern section embodies thick, strongly articulated, and sharply curved sternpost, of which tip is missing. Hollow thwartships tube near stern, open to either side of vessel,

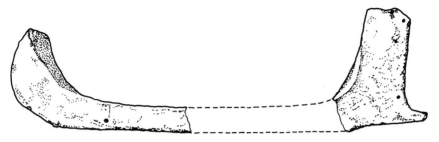

BA 25. Drawing by Frederick and Caroline Hemans, after Petrakos, 1974.

served to hold an axle to which wheels were originally attached to pull model along ground.

BA 26. Boat model from Asine.

Late Mycenaean (Hagg)

Mycenaean (Göttlicher)

Burial offering (?)

Restored L: ca. 15 cm

Nauplion, Nauplion Archaeological Museum 3352

Göttlicher, 1978:63, no. 332, pl. 25 (shows model intact, wrongly); Hagg, in the work of Wachsmann, 1982:299–302.

Fragmentary buff-colored clay model of planked small craft. One end and section of hull preserved; remainder missing. Details in reddish-brown paint. Horizontal painted bands along exterior at top, center, and bottom represent gunwale or cap rail, strake or strake joint, and keel, respectively. Preserved end has slightly hooked ter-

BA 26. Photograph by the author.

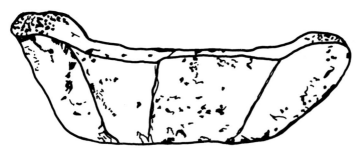

BA 27. Drawing by the author, after Göttlicher, 1978.

minal at top of angular stempost or sternpost. On interior, four transverse painted bands represent frames, indicating that model is of small craft. Curved or rockered keel.

BA 27. Boat model from Kapari (near Phylakopi), Melos.
Prehistoric (?)
Findspot unknown
L: 26.5 cm; H: 6.5 cm
Melos, Melos Museum

Fraser, 1969–27, fig. 31; Göttlicher, 1978:60, no. 311, pl. 24; Laviosa, 1969–70:29, fig. 28; *Papadopoulou-Zapheiropoulou, 1966:386–87, pl. 408 γ–δ.

    Fragmentary limestone model of flat-bottomed boat. Portions of sides and gunwale missing; one side restored. One end (stern?) slightly higher than other; higher end at slightly steeper angle to bottom than lower end. In plan, both ends are pointed. On bottom, longitudinal axial incised line and two thicker transverse incised lines may represent keel and frames, respectively.

3

Geometric Period

Six of the eight (or possibly more) ship and boat models from the Geometric period are from Crete; furthermore, the only two examples from the mainland (Geom. 2 and 3) comprise a single paired find from the same context. This distribution pattern recalls that of the Early and Middle Bronze Ages, in which most models were from Crete. Future finds are unlikely to change the pattern for the Geometric period, since so many more mainland than Cretan sites of the Geometric period have already been excavated.

Only one of the Geometric models is even tentatively dated to before the Late Geometric period (Geom. 1).[1] The remainder are all dated by their excavators to the Late Geometric period or slightly later. This reemergence of ship models more or less conforms to the return of ship representations in other media, especially those on the Late Geometric I Dipylon group of funerary vases.[2]

Architecture

Although far fewer representations of watercraft have been preserved from the Geometric period than from the Late Bronze Age, enough material remains from the Late Geometric period to indicate continuity in ship architecture. This is most evident in the characteristic projecting forefoot in Bronze Age ships, which reemerges in the Late Geometric period on both painted and modeled vessels.[3] This forefoot, which in the Bronze Age projects slightly forward beyond the stempost and is generally interpreted as a keel extension of uncertain function, becomes longer in the Geometric period, as do the hulls of ships in general.[4] In painted representations of Geometric ships, the forefoot may either curve upward from the keel or project horizontally in a straight line, continuing the line of the keel.[5] Normally, long oared galleys are depicted in Late Geometric ship representations; occasionally, they are rigged with a sail.[6] With one exception (Geom. 1), Geometric models similarly depict oared galleys with slim, elongated proportions; none, however, are equipped with masts or sails or any of the associated rigging.[7] Thus Geom. 2–4 preserve the projecting forefoot and closed-in bow compartment with upwardly curving stempost so common in painted representations. Additionally, Geom. 2 and 3 display the characteristic curved sternpost of the period and may be the earliest ships to show the theriomorphic goose head decoration on that member,[8] although the degree of corrosion leaves this feature ambiguous. None of the forefeet of the models project as far forward beyond the stempost as those of the painted representations do, although the relative shortness of the forefeet on Geom. 2–4 may again be the result of extensive corrosion. On Geom. 6, the forefoot projects so little that the effect is that of a bifid bow, in which the upper surface of the bow compartment projects as far forward as the forefoot. Although the forefeet visible on Late Geometric ship models are longer and more massive than their Bronze Age counterparts, it is perhaps too early to label them rams,[9] especially when Homer is silent on the subject and the ramming tactic is absent from the few pictorial sea battles of the Geometric period.[10]

Of the Geometric models, only Geom. 6 has a crew. In it are seated five rowers facing aft, the lower portions of their bodies cut off by the gunwale or cap rail. The artist emphasized the latter feature by horizontally projecting it beyond the edge of the port side.[11] The relative shallowness of the hull indicates that the ship is an aphract, or open undecked galley,[12] although the vessel's height may be due in part to its function as an attachment of a larger object. This would also account for the small size of the vessel, indicated by the small number of rowers: at 5 per side, there would be a total of 10 rowers. The smallest number of rowers mentioned by Homer is 20.[13]

Unlike Geom. 2–6, which conform to the standard oared galleys depicted upon contemporary pottery, Geom. 1 appears to represent the small craft tradition for the period. It is the only depiction of a round ship with a flat bottom, either painted or modeled, from the entire Geometric period, and as such it is of considerable architectural interest. Its small size is shown by the presence of only nine frames on the interior and by the comparatively large scale of the occupant relative to the length and beam of the hull. Two horizontal painted bands around the hull's exterior, ending on either side at the stern, delineate either strakes or the joints between strakes and the gunwale or cap rail. They continue unbroken around the rounded bow; along the port side they are connected by a thick diagonal painted line, which may portray a scarf joint. There is no indication of a stempost or a keel on the vessel's exterior, of which the flat bottom is unpainted. On the interior, three axial longitudinal lines, straddled by the crewman, represent the edges of two limber strakes flanking or superimposed over the keel, the spaces between the lines depicting the limber strakes (or possibly ceiling planks) themselves. Similar partial interior planking is known from later shipwrecks, such as the Kyrenia ship.[14] Outboard of these lines are short thwartships lines and spaces that delineate the frames. There are ten on the starboard side and at least six to port.[15] Approximately evenly spaced, the frames end near the crewman's feet. The upper ends of most frames terminate against another horizontal line, which may represent either a clamp or, as seems likelier, the gunwale. At least two frames on the starboard side and at least one to port continue through this line up to the rail, serving as rail stanchions. The space between the gunwale and cap rail appears to have been left open. The rail itself is depicted as a painted band which is interrupted on either side by six holes and at the bow by one hole. These holes would have served as suspension holes for hanging the model, as attachment places for forestay and shrouds,[16] or as oarports and a hawsehole. A small hole in the boat's "forefoot" probably would have held a line for pulling the model along the ground.[17] The area behind the sailor is open and may originally have had a rounded stern, or possibly a transom, since the area appears to be slightly flattened.[18] From an architectural perspective, Geom. 1 is extremely complex, especially considering Brock's placement of it in the Protogeometric B period. However, a similar model from Cyprus is dated even earlier, to the Late Bronze Age.[19] Morrison and Williams attempt with limited success to relate the architecture of Geom. 1 to the warships on the Dipylon vases;[20] however, the comparison is somewhat irrelevant since Geom. 1 is a Cretan small craft and not an Attic warship.

Functions

Geom. 1–5 all derive from funerary contexts, and served as burial offerings, at least at the time of their deposit. Brock stated in passing his belief that Geom. 1, found along with other miniature objects, must have been a child's toy at one time.[21] However, the disturbed context of the tomb in which Geom. 1 was found precludes any certainty as to its primary function before its service as a burial offering.

Geom. 2 and 3 from Argos and Geom. 4 and 5 from Kavousi,

Crete, represent pairs of firedogs in the form of warships. Each pair came from a single grave, each of which also included spits. Three similar pairs of ship-shaped firedogs have been found in contemporary or slightly later graves on Cyprus, at Kouklia (Palaipaphos), Patriki, and Salamis.[22] J. Boardman supports P. Courbin in interpreting these items as valued objects taken from among the private possessions of the deceased to be placed in his grave.[23] Conversely, V. Karageorghis supports W. Deonna in interpreting the firedogs as metaphysical vehicles for transporting the soul of the dead to the afterworld.[24] However, since all five burials were of single individuals, in every case a single firedog would have sufficed for the hypothetical mystical-symbolic journey. Yet in all five tombs on Crete and Cyprus, the firedogs were found in pairs. This suggests that they served some other function that required a matched pair. That function is indicated by the presence of large numbers of iron spits in all five tombs: the firedogs served as a base across which spits could be stretched to roast food. The food could either be skewered on the spits or, if too large, be laid across the spits like a grill.[25] No satisfactory symbolic explication has yet been proposed for the combined presence of the spits and the firedogs. Therefore, the use of Geom. 2–5 as burial offerings appears to have been a secondary use, after their primary use as objects of daily life.

In view of the fact that the Argos firedogs are the earliest manifestations of the ship-shaped brazier, it seems likely that the form originated in mainland Greece in the late eighth century B.C. and rapidly passed to Crete and Cyprus within a single generation, after which it disappeared.[26] Courbin's theory that the deceased may have been a mariner is not supported by any evidence from within the graves themselves, although there is perhaps some tenuous mythical or symbolic connection between ships and monumental funerary vases of the Late Geometric I Dipylon and later periods.[27] The presence of an unknown number of Geometric boat models from the sanctuary at Inatos on Crete indicates a continuity of function from the Bronze Age, at least for Crete.

Geom. 2–6 mark the earliest use of three-dimensional ship representations as subordinate elements of larger objects: Geom 2–5 are ship-shaped firedogs, and Geom. 6 is part of the decoration of a cauldron stand.[28] Here, as is true of some later examples and painted representations of all periods, the size and proportions of the ship depend to a large extent on the medium and size of the space to be filled rather than on the skill of the artist, artisan, or sculptor. Inevitably, the subsidiary nautical motif is distorted in favor of the primary object that it embellishes. Thus, for instance, the ship portions of Geom. 2–5 are limited to the ends of the firedogs only, while the hulls and overall proportions are totally distorted in order to allow the firedogs to serve as cooking utensils. Similarly, Geom. 6, a small subsidiary decorative element of a cauldron stand, was cast by means of the à jour technique, which yields by definition an almost two-dimensionally flat product. This renders invalid any discussion of the ship's overall proportions and beam or other topics. Unfortunately, while deformation of an object's nautical attributes is usually discernible, the degree of misrepresentation usually is not, since comparable renderings of ships or their parts in other media are just as distorted or even more so.

CATALOG

Geom. 1. Boat model from Tomb X, Fortetsa cemetery (Crete).
Protogeometric B (*Brock)
Protogeometric B–Late Geometric
Burial offering
L: 11 cm; B: 6.5 cm; H: 2.5 cm
Heraklion, Heraklion Museum

*Brock, 1957:41–43, 53, 143, pl. 36 (three views); Göttlicher, 1978:63, no. 327; Gray, 1974:G21, no. D 2; Morrison, in the work of Greenhill, 1976:159, fig. 110; Morrison and Williams, 1968:17, pl. 1f; Snodgrass, 1971:82–83.

Geom. 1. Courtesy of Prof. John S. Morrison.

Buff clay model of undecked flat-bottomed small craft, with details in dark brown varnish. Unrestored; small portions missing along rail and on interior. Two horizontal painted bands around outside of hull delineate strakes or strake joints and gunwale or cap rail, respectively. Portside strakes connected by diagonal line, possibly a scarf. Flat bottom rough and unpainted. Inside, three axial longitudinal lines represent limber strakes or ceiling. Short thwartships lines represent frames. Above frames are two longitudinal lines for gunwale and cap rail. Frames extending above gunwale terminate at rail and portray rail stanchions. Hole in forefoot probably string hole for dragging model along ground. Hole at upper surface of bow possibly hawsehole or hole for forestay. Six holes along each rail served either as oarports or as holes for attachment of shrouds or suspension lines. Painted male figurine with arms on rail occupies open-ended stern; probably represents helmsman.

Geom. 2 and 3. Pair of firedogs (andirons) in form of warships, from Warrior's Grave, Argos.

Late Geometric

Burial offerings (secondary)

F10 restored L: 1.295 m; H (without legs): 15.4 cm (at bow), 16.2 cm (at stern)

F11 restored L: 1.34 m; H (without legs): 10.2 cm (at bow), 15 cm (at stern)

Argos, Argos Museum F10, F11

Boardman, 1971:6–8, fig. 1; Courbin, 1956:172; *1957:322–86, with several figures; Deonna, 1959b:247–53, with remarks by Courbin; Göttlicher, 1978:64, nos. 338–39, pl. 25; Gray, 1974:G24, no. G 12; Karageorghis, 1963a:272, n. 2, 292, nn. 1, 2, 293–94; Kopcke, 1967:146; Kurtz and Boardman, 1971:203, 207–8.

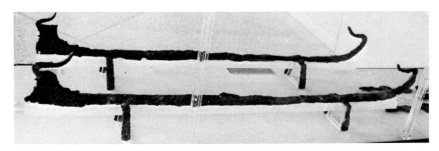

Geom. 2 and 3. Photograph by the author.

Pair of forged iron firedogs in the form of war galleys. Forefoot and portions of center bar of F10 missing. Stempost and portions of center bar of F11 missing. All surfaces corroded. Slender, very attenuated proportions. Bow compartments have two horizontal raised ridges, possibly representing wales. Stems incorporate short forefeet, exaggeratedly large bow compartments, and S-curved stemposts characteristic of war galleys painted on Geometric pottery. Sterns possibly decorated with goose heads and necks, curving upward and facing into hull of vessels. Stems and sterns connected by long iron bars, which represent schematic hulls. Feet are pairs of flat iron strips in inverted-U form.

Geom. 4 and 5. Pair of firedogs (andirons) in form of warships, from grave (tholos tomb?) at Kavousi, Crete.

Ca. 700 B.C. (*Boardman)

Late Geometric

Burial offerings (secondary)

Dimensions unpublished

Heraklion, Heraklion Museum (possibly missing)

*Boardman, 1971:5–8, pl. δ'; Göttlicher, 1978:62, no. 322; Kurtz and Boardman, 1971:208.

Pair of iron firedogs in the form of war galleys. Four fragments preserved; all surfaces badly corroded. Largest fragment comprises bow compartment, forefoot and curved stempost, one pair of feet, and short section of hull. Other three fragments incorporate portions of feet and short section of central bar (representing schematized hull) to either side. Feet are in form of inverted U, as on Geom. 2 and 3.

Geom. 6. Cauldron stand decoration in form of warship, from Idaean Cave, Crete.

Early Bronze Age? (Göttlicher)

Geometric (Boardman, S. Casson, Dohan, Karo)

Late Geometric–Post-Geometric (Rolley)

Post-Geometric (Gray, Kirk, Morrison and Williams)

Greco-Archaic (Maraghiannis)

Votive

Dimensions unpublished

Heraklion, Heraklion Museum

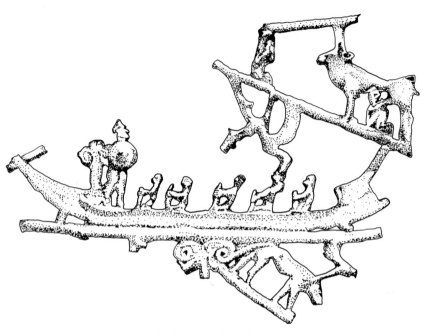

Geom. 6. Drawing by Frederick and Caroline Hemans, after Boardman, 1961.

Alexiou, 1958:282, pl. 1 δ′, fig. 1; Boardman, 1961:132–34, fig. 49a; S. Casson, 1933:47, fig. 18; Dohan, 1930–31:212, fig. 3; Göttlicher, 1978:61, no. 312; Gray, 1974:G25, no. H 2; Karo, 1920:132–33; Kirk, 1949:116, n. 29; Maraghiannis, 1911–15:VIII, pl. XLII; Marinatos, 1933:199; Moll, 1929:B I 37; Morrison and Williams, 1968: 79, Arch. 26; *Orsi, 1888:729–30, fig. 1; Rolley, 1975:157, figs. 1–2.

Cast bronze, à jour style. Model of small aphract warship, originally forming part of decoration of larger bronze object, probably a cauldron stand (Boardman). Fashioned to be viewed only on port side. Low, attenuated proportions, with shallow hull, large bow compartment, and high undecorated stern. Flat bottom, stem and stern rising in gradual curve from keel. Forefoot squared at end, possibly an indication of attachments now missing. Similarly, reinforcing bar at stern may also represent steering oar. Gunwale or cap rail marked by horizontally projecting strip from beginning of curve at stern to after edge of bow compartment. On gunwale or cap rail are placed five rowers facing aft, wielding oars. Bodies are visible from knees upward, an indication that vessel is undecked. In stern area are two figures on a larger scale than the rowers: a man (marine?) armed with round bossed shield and a slender, skirted woman with upper arms against body and forearms raised. Mythical possibilities for two larger figures in stern include Ariadne and Theseus, Helen and Menelaos voyaging from Crete to Egypt, or Helen abducted by Paris (Alexiou). Technique and style are consistent with Late Geometric period (or early seventh century B.C.), although boat type appears slightly later; these differences account for the wide disparity in dates.

Geom. 7. Boat model from sanctuary at Inatos, Crete.
Geometric
Votive
Dimensions unpublished
Heraklion, Heraklion Museum 13272

Unpublished. Mentioned by Alexiou, 1976:205; Göttlicher, 1978:63, no. 326; Laviosa, 1969–70:29, n. 3.

"Has a mast attachment at the center" (Laviosa).

Geom. 8–?. Boat models from sanctuary at Inatos, Crete.
Geometric
Votives
Dimensions unpublished
Heraklion, Heraklion Museum

Unpublished. Mentioned by Alexiou, 1976:205; Göttlicher, 1978: 62, no. 325; Laviosa, 1969–70:29, n. 3; Price, 1978:86–87; Tyree, 1974:32, 285.

Alexiou and Laviosa refer to more than one model from Inatos; neither gives exact numbers. Tyree mentions "several clay boats," adding that one is of coarse orange clay (length: ca. 25 cm) with two seats, something in the bottom and third and fourth seats possibly missing. Another is of coarse pink clay (length: ca. 24 cm) and is dated to the Archaic period (?).

4

Archaic Period

The number of ship and boat models produced during the Archaic period increased markedly; at least 53 examples, or more than six times the number from the Geometric period, have been found. The number of watercraft representations in other contemporary forms of artwork increased as well, especially in vase painting. However, in terms of the geographical distribution of the Archaic models, these figures are somewhat misleading, since most models are clustered at only a few sites. These include 17 from Corinth, 22 from the Heraion of Samos, 3 from Ischia off mainland Italy, and 2 each from Athens and Boeotia. In addition, single examples have been found in Greece at Perachora, Isthmia, and Delos and in Anatolia at Larisa on the Hermos and Sardis. Only one so-called Archaic model, in a private collection in Switzerland, is from a completely unknown context (Arch. 49, a possible fake).

Architecture

Unlike their contemporary painted counterparts, the published Archaic watercraft models are comparatively uninformative from an architectural perspective.[1] Nine of the models are fragmentary, comprising only the bow, the stern, or a short section of the hull (Arch. 7–9, 23, 24, 29, 31, 33, and 52). In these cases (excepting Arch. 23), it is not possible to determine whether they represent warships, merchant vessels, or small craft. Another six pieces appear to represent small craft (Arch. 1, 25, 45, 46, 49, and 52), as is shown by either the low length-to-beam ratio, the small number of frames, or the small number of rowers. In all of the cases where small craft are represented, the bottoms (or keels) are strongly rockered, although the ends may be either rounded or angular. One small craft model from the Archaic period has small decks at bow and stern (Arch. 49); all of the others are undecked.

Among the Archaic models, only one may be even tentatively identified as a merchant vessel by its rounded proportions and relatively great depth (Arch. 14).[2] Although less than half of one side and a short section of the keel are preserved, Arch. 14 is of considerable importance, since it is the only extant example from the ancient world of a built model, constructed of separate pieces of wood for the keel and sides. Small circular and rectangular holes in the midsection of the preserved hull fragment indicate that originally there were additional details, possibly thwarts, benches, and other appurtenances, which have not survived.[3] However, enough remains to indicate that the keel was strongly rockered. In addition, the angle of the joint between the keel and side shows that in section the sides of the hull were steeper and straighter than might be expected from an examination of contemporary representations in other media and later shipwrecks.

The remaining intact and fragmentary models from the Archaic period represent warships. The 22 models from the Samian Heraion, the largest contemporary group from a single context, are architecturally uniform, with low, slender proportions. Their forms presumably result from having been carved from single blocks of wood. The maximum beam for all but 6 of the Samian pieces is only 3 centimeters, although the preserved lengths vary from 28 to 51.9 centimeters. The length-to-beam ratio for these ships, therefore, varies between 10:1 and 19.2:1, and would have been even greater when the models were intact.[4] The lower ratio (10:1) matches the estimated proportions of the standard Athenian *trieres*, based upon the fourth century B.C. ship sheds in Athens.[5] Where the bottoms of the Samian models are preserved, they are usually curved in profile, an indication that the keels were rockered. Two examples (Arch. 10 and 17) have articulated keels, rectangular or rounded in section, carved on their bottoms. The forefeet (rams?) of the Samian warships are consistently portrayed not as linear horizontal keel extensions, but as a gradual curve rising from the rockered keel at the waterline. This feature is similar to the curving forefeet on the Late Geometric Dipylon warships and the later Early Protoattic krater in Toronto,[6] which may be broadly dated from the last quarter of the eighth century B.C. to the first quarter of the seventh century B.C.[7] The majority of the Samian models are flat on their uppermost surface; from this it may be inferred that they depict decked vessels. However, Arch. 10, 11, and 17 have longitudinal grooves or channels along their upper surface, triangular in section, which must represent the hollow interior of an undecked ship. There is no internal evidence that any of the Samian models represent ships with more than a single bank of rowers; the low height of most of them would seem to indicate the simpler one-level warship.

The only additional architectural feature preserved on any of the Samian wooden models is a series of 20 small broken wooden pegs or dowels vertically set into the deck of Arch. 13. Sixteen of these are set at regular intervals in opposed pairs along the length of the gunwales; an additional pair is found on the rising portion of the sternpost, and one each at the highest point of the bow compartment and the sternpost. D. Ohly and Göttlicher considered these to be tholepins for an 18-oared ship, or possibly rail stanchions.[8] However, it seems equally likely in light of the single pegs at bow and stern and the extreme 20:1 proportions of the vessel that they might have held some form of superstructure, such as additional planking, spray screens, or even another deck level. There is no evidence for masts or sails on any of the Samian models. Of the group, only Arch. 10 from the mid seventh century B.C. and Arch. 15–24 from the second half of the seventh century are from datable contexts; the remainder are tentatively dated to the same period through their stylistic similarities.[9]

Theriomorphic rams on warships first appear in wall paintings, reliefs, and models in the Archaic period. Prior to this, during the Geometric period, only long forefeet appear as flat pointed appurtenances on the bows of oared galleys.[10] It is possible that the concept of the theriomorphic ram terminal developed from the placement of the apotropaic or pathfinding oculus at the bow of a ship, as first seen in the Bronze Age (on BA 20). This feature does not appear during the Geometric period, although the large spoked "wagon wheel" commonly set in the bow compartment of Geometric galleys may have served as a stylized oculus.[11] Alternatively, the "wagon wheel" may have been an ensign, or a schematized shield for the bow lookout. A shield does appear in an oculuslike opening at the stern of at least one Geometric warship,[12] and in one instance an oculus is decorated with two concentric circles, like a shield boss.[13] The eye, which reappears during the Archaic period in the first half of the seventh century, is depicted more naturalistically than it is during preceding periods.[14] With one possible exception,[15] it no longer appears in the bow compartment, but is now placed lower in the ship's structure, at the base of the ram, where it remains for the duration of the Archaic period and later.[16] Given the purpose of the ram to hole or gore the adversary's hull, it might naturally follow that the realistic eye would evolve into a boar's head decoration for the ram itself.

Rams embellished with eyes appear upon models at the same time as or slightly later than they do upon ship depictions in other media. When present, they are set at the base of the ram, as they are on Arch. 30, or at the base of the stempost, as they are on Arch. 2, which is slightly earlier. On Arch. 30, the earliest model on which the ram is preserved, the ram is blunted at its tip.

Arch. 30 is the most elaborate ship model from the Archaic period. Each individual timber in the bow compartment is delineated by a separate line, and the structure is topped by a raked stempost originally similar to that of Arch. 2. Inside the bow compartment, the remains of a thwart are visible; this may have supported the figure of a crew member[17] or was possibly intended to represent a cathead.[18] A low axial ridge along the model's deck either may have resulted from the modeling of the rhyton[19] or may correspond to the sloping deck of a modern ship, which allows water to run off the deck.[20] The stern is bounded by a thick rail to either side, decorated like the bow compartment with lines representing either studs or stanchions. Between these rails sits a helmsman with his hands upon his knees, in a casual attitude similar to that of the sailor in Geom. 1. Behind, the sternpost and pouring spout for the rhyton are integrated into a high, curved member rising from the vessel's underbody.[21] A guilloche pattern of reversed sigmas alternating with dots along both sides of the rhyton may serve either as a simple decorative motif or possibly as a stylized wave pattern at the waterline. Other painted details are almost certainly decorative and not architectural in intent.

Arch. 32, a kyathos or kantharos, resembles Arch. 30 in that both are pouring or drinking vessels from Boeotia with decorative naval attributes. In place of one of its handles, Arch. 32 incorporates the ram, stempost, and bow compartment of a warship. Although it is approximately a century later in date, Arch. 32 has a blunted ram tip resembling that of Arch. 30. In keeping with contemporary vase paintings and representations in other media, the ram is now fully theriomorphic, with boar's tusk, mouth, jowl markings, and eye and brow.[22] The bow compartment also closely resembles the corresponding structure on Arch. 30, in that it is decorated by closely set vertical painted lines representing framework. However, the stempost is decorated only by a solid black glaze. The handle opposite the ship's prow is further endowed with nautical iconography in the form of a long spur near the point of attachment to the vase's body, which may portray the steering oar. Moreover, the finial at the top of the handle, which is a feature common on Attic kyathoi,[23] is surmounted by an apotropaic oculus rather than the normal Attic knob. The recurved form of the handle itself also resembles the characteristic goose head decoration of sternposts on contemporary painted warships.[24] These specific naval attributes are further emphasized by the presence on the vessel's rim of leaping fish, a Triton figure, and winged sirens. Similar motifs decorate Arch. 49.

Multiple crewmen (as opposed to passengers) appear more frequently aboard models from the Archaic period than they do previously. Crew members are unknown on models from the Bronze Age Aegean, although they appear frequently aboard contemporary Egyptian models and on one Bronze Age Cypriote model.[25] Only two Geometric models[26] have crews, although they are commonly depicted in contemporary vase paintings.[27] In the Cypriote model, in Geom. 1, and in Arch. 30, the crew is limited to a single individual seated in the vessel's stern, his hands either upon his knees or along the gunwale. Although the attitude of the crewman is passive and unconnected to any shipboard activity in all three examples, he is usually thought to be the helmsman because of his placement in the stern.[28] Arch. 46, 48, and 49 have multiple crews on board of four, five, and seven individuals, respectively. The crewmen on Arch. 48 are again passive; their shields possibly identify them as marines rather than sailors, although the central individual is playing the double flute and may be the vessel's *auletes*.[29] Arch. 46 has four crewmen, including two rowers in the boat's center plying their oars over the gunwales and single individuals at bow and stern. Each of the single figures has his left arm folded across his midsection and his right arm slightly raised, as if exhorting the rowers to greater effort.[30] Arch. 49 (a possible fake) has the largest crew in any Archaic model. The crew consists of six rowers in three pairs and a helmsman at the stern. All of the crew figurines are removable, a fact that may explain why the rowers are facing the wrong direction (toward the bow).[31] That the crew are rowers and not paddlers is indicated by the three oarports along the gunwale and the position of the crew's hands. The helmsman at the stern of Arch. 49 is of a different (smaller) scale than are the rowers and may not belong with the original ensemble.[32] Both of the Archaic models that have active crew members (Arch. 46 and 49) are small craft, with theriomorphic attributes attached to one end of the craft: either an animal protome, as on the bow of Arch. 46, or a fishtail, as on the stern of Arch. 49.

Aside from these examples from the Archaic period, Greek (and Roman) watercraft models seldom include members of the crew.[33] The inclusion of crewmen in models is far more popular in Cyprus from the Bronze Age onward, especially during the Cypro-Archaic period.[34]

Functions

Of the 31 Archaic boat models for which specific proveniences are known, only Arch. 1 is a burial offering. This is a reversal from the Geometric period, when most models were from burials. However, the original function of Arch. 1 is questionable, since a long spout midway along the hull indicates that at one time the vessel was used for pouring or drinking a liquid.[35] Its use as a burial offering may be a secondary rather than a primary function. Two other spouted vessels in the form of boats, Arch. 30 and 32, may also have served either ritual or domestic functions.[36] If they served as burial offerings, they may have been modeled specifically for funerary libations or banquets, or they may simply have been prized possessions of the deceased. The early Lydian inscription on Arch. 1, executed before the model was fired, seems to include three names; however, since the inscription is as yet untranslated, it is uncertain whether the names are human or divine.[37]

The remaining 30 models from known proveniences are without exception votives. As was mentioned above, this is a reversal from the Geometric period.[38] Twenty-two of the 30 are wooden models from the Heraion of Samos and are perhaps to be associated with the mid seventh century B.C. flood of the area, or the postflood replacement of the Hera temple and its aniconic wooden cult statue. One of the models was found in a mid seventh century riverbed deposit in the sacred precinct.[39] On the basis of the crudity of workmanship and durability of material, G. Kopcke has suggested that these models were carved at or near the Heraion and then dedicated by a victorious warship crew, possibly as a tithe of the victory booty.[40]

If the models were carved by sailors, as seems likely in view of their uniform crudity, several motives are possible, aside from the one offered by Kopcke, for their having been dedicated at the Heraion. The dedicants may simply have been citizens or sailors of Samos who survived a calamity at sea or wished to prevent one. Alternatively, the sailors may have been citizens of any state who won or survived a sea battle near Samos and wished to honor the local goddess. It is also possible that by the Archaic period, Hera of Samos was a specific patron deity of seafarers. Certainly, Samos had been a naval power from the late eighth century B.C., when Corinth built four warships for her Samian allies in the Lelantine War.[41] Samos had also participated in overseas commercial ventures or settlements in Tartessus in Spain and Naucratis in Egypt,[42] and was one of the major maritime powers in Greece during the Age of the Tyrants in the late Archaic period.[43] The Samians dedicated a large bronze krater to Hera upon their return from the discovery of Tartessus;[44] the wooden ship votives may embody a similar motive, or might be ritual votives rather than individual gifts.[45] Whatever the original motive, by the end of the seventh century B.C., Hera of Samos was a primary maritime deity. Aside from the wooden models, an actual full-sized warship was dedicated in the sanctuary to Hera and Poseidon around 600 B.C. and was placed along the access road from the altar to the basin.[46] In addition, a fragmentary inscription of the sixth century B.C. from the Heraion refers to the dedication to Hera and Poseidon of no fewer than seven ships by an individual named Amphidemos.[47]

An analogous clustering of models exists at Corinth, where 17 models of watercraft have been found dating from the Archaic period. Of this number, however, only three are from precise geographical or chronological contexts (Arch. 25, 31, and 47); the remainder have only generalized proveniences of the "Potters' Quarter" or "Corinth." Since a large number of the models were found in the Potters' Quarter, it may be presumed that they were manufactured there, as one of a variety of popular terracotta objects produced by the local craftsmen. As was the situation in Samos, the models probably reflect Corinth's interest and participation in maritime affairs, which date from the colonization period in the eighth century B.C. According to Stillwell, Arch 52, from a votive context at Perachora, was manufactured at Corinth; since it and two of the Corinthian models (Arch. 31 and 47) were found in votive contexts, it may be suggested but not proved that similar functions were intended for the other examples.[48]

One new function for watercraft models has been attributed to the Archaic period. At Delos, a trapezoidal stone block, which served as an Archaic votive statue base, was found in the vicinity of the Hellenistic Sanctuary of the Bulls.[49] It is decorated with a ram's head on its smaller end and with gorgon masks on two other surfaces. P. Couchoud and J. Svoronos identify these features as ship's devices; on this basis and in light of the presence on the base's surface of a graffito of a ship's stern, they further identify the base as the earliest manifestation of a statue base in the form of a ship's prow.[50] J. Marcadé supported this hypothesis and dated the base to the end of the seventh century B.C., presumably on the basis of the letter forms of the dedicatory inscription.[51] However, contrary to the conclusions of Couchoud and Svoronos,[52] ship's devices of any sort are unknown among ancient watercraft representations before the late Hellenistic or Roman Republican periods; Couchoud and Svoronos probably conflated the ram's head with the more common boar's head ram terminal, or possibly even the goose head *cheniskos* that frequently decorates sternposts of the Archaic and later periods.[53] On the basis of the information now available, the earliest statue base in the form of a warship prow has been dated to the Hellenistic period, as will be seen in chapter 6.

CATALOG

Arch. 1. Boat model from square chamber tomb, eastern slope of Necropolis Hill, Sardis.

Ca. 700 B.C. (Göttlicher)

7th century B.C. (Bossert)

600–550 B.C. (Gusmani)

Burial offering (secondary)

L: 30.5 cm; B: 14 cm; L:B ratio: 2.2:1

Princeton, Princeton Art Museum 29-195

Bossert, 1942:27, no. 197, pl. 34.197; Göttlicher, 1978:23, no. 1; Gusmani, 1964:16, 21, 262, no. 30; Littman, 1916:56–57, with figures of inscription.

Boat model of micaceous clay; probably small craft. In profile, ends are strongly rockered, terminating in points. Bow and stern are identical and of equal height. Long, thin spout emerges from middle of one side, rising to just above gunwale. To right of spout, a two-line verse inscription in Lydian, added prior to firing.[54] Untranslated,

Arch. 1. Courtesy of The Art Museum, Princeton University, Princeton, New Jersey. Gift of the Sardis Excavation Society.

the inscription is transcribed by Gusmani:

titisin:emv·tisardv:fabil ataλ·kitvaλ

Littman interprets last two words as proper names in oblique case, with genitive meaning, but is uncertain whether names are human or divine.[55] Gusmani considers the inscription to be a dedication.[56]

Arch. 2. Stempost of boat model from Larisa on the Hermos.
700–660 B.C.
Function unknown
H: ca. 9.5 cm
Izmir, Izmir Museum (?)
*Boehlau and Schefold, 1942:90, fig. 29, pl. 38.15

Fragmentary stempost of clay warship model; details added in paint.[57] Broken off at bottom; remainder (of ship) missing. Manufactured locally.[58] Four zones of decoration separated by four horizontal lines. At top, thick horizontal painted band; beneath is a pair of dots in reserved squares. Second zone comprises slenderly proportioned animals, probably dogs, looking backward over their shoulders. Dog on port side looks forward; dog on starboard side looks aft. Third zone has a soldier bird with reserved body to either

Arch. 2. Drawing by the author, after Boehlau and Schefold, 1942.

side and floral motifs above and below. Fourth and lowest zone has oculus to either side, with dot iris and reserved pupil. Below oculus to port is a concentric triangle motif, broken off at bottom. By analogy with Arch. 18 and 20, this stempost would have decorated the bow of an extremely large model, originally perhaps 50 centimeters long.

Arch. 3. Ship model from area 014, Heraion of Samos.
Mid 7th century B.C.
Votive
Preserved L: 37.3 cm; B: 2.6 cm; H: 5.8 cm (bow); preserved L:B ratio: 14:1
Samos, Vathy Museum H 83

Göttlicher, 1978:65, no. 345, pl. 25; Gray, 1974:G26, no. H 17, G58, G90; *Kopcke, 1967:145–46, fig. 20, no. 46, pl. 82, 1–2.

   Wooden model of warship, carved from single piece of wood. Stern, tip of ram, and top of bow compartment missing. Hole near stern due to missing wood knot; surface of hull very rough and knotty. Very long, slender proportions, with proportionately oversized bow compartment. Keel slightly rockered along hull, rising steeply at bow. Ram at higher level than keel. Flat, smoothly finished deck.

Arch. 4. Ship model from area 014, Heraion of Samos.
Mid 7th century B.C.
Votive
Preserved L: 36.8 cm; B: 2.5 cm; H: 5.1 cm (stern); preserved L:B ratio: 14.2:1
Samos, Vathy Museum H 84

Göttlicher, 1978:65, no. 342, pl. 25; Gray, 1974:G26, no. H 17, G58, G90, *Kopcke, 1967:145–46, no. 47, fig. 20, pl. 82, 3–4.

   Wooden model of warship, carved from single block of wood. Stern, ram, top of bow compartment, and lower edge of ram missing. Hull surface very rough, with worm hole along port gunwale. Long, slender proportions. Keel slightly rockered, with stem and stern curving strongly upward. Flat deck, with steps to bow compartment and stern.

Arch. 5. Ship model from area 014, Heraion of Samos.
Mid 7th century B.C.

Votive

Preserved L: 28 cm; B: 2.7 cm (deck); H: 3.9 cm (midships); preserved L:B ratio: 10.4:1

Samos, Vathy Museum H 85

Göttlicher, 1978:65, no. 343, pl. 25; Gray, 1974:G26, no. H 17, G58, G90, *Kopcke, 1967:145–46, no. 48, fig. 20, no. 48, pl. 83, 1.

Wooden model of warship, carved from single block of wood. Tip of stern, bow and ram, and small portions along keel missing. Knot holes through deck, hull, keel, stern, and bow compartment; surface of deck and hull otherwise smooth. Slender, elongated proportions. Keel slightly rockered, curving sharply upward at stern; bow compartment smaller and better proportioned than on Arch. 3. Flat deck.

Arch. 6. Ship model from area 014, Heraion of Samos.
Mid 7th century B.C.

Votive

Preserved L: 27.3 cm; B: 2.7 cm (deck); H: 3.2 cm (midships); preserved L:B ratio: 10.1:1

Samos, Vathy Museum H 86

Göttlicher, 1978:65, no. 344, pl. 25; Gray, 1974:G26, no. H 17, G58, G90; *Kopcke, 1967:145–46, no. 49, fig. 20, no. 49, pl. 83, 2.

Wooden warship model, carved from single block of wood. Stern, tip of ram missing. Deck surface smooth, hull sides rough. Slender, attenuated proportions. In section, starboard side of hull is concave, rather than convex, as is normal. Flat keel rises at bow to ram. Bow compartment small, merging into ram.

Arch. 7. Fragment of ship model from area 014, Heraion of Samos.
Mid 7th century B.C.

Votive

Preserved L: 10.3 cm

Samos, Vathy Museum H 87

Göttlicher, 1978:64–65, no. 341; Gray, 1974:G26, no. H 17, G58, G90; *Kopcke, 1967:145, 148, no. 50, pl. 83, 3 left.

Small, badly preserved fragment of wooden boat model (warship?). Possibly the bow, since it incorporates a slight rise at the thinner end. Surface badly abraded. Göttlicher and Kopcke consider it a stern fragment.

Arch. 8. Boat model from area 014, Heraion of Samos.
Mid 7th century B.C.
Votive
Preserved L: 12 cm; B: 2.5 cm; H: 4.5 cm
Samos, Vathy Museum H 88

Göttlicher, 1978:64, no. 340; Gray, 1974:G26, no. H 17, G58, G90; *Kopcke, 1967:145, 148, no. 51, pl. 83, 3 right.

Small, badly preserved fragment of bark boat model (warship?). Surface badly abraded. Short section of hull preserved, remainder missing. Preserved hull section indicates flat keel, with high, up-curving stern.

Arch. 9. Boat model from area 014, Heraion of Samos.
Mid 7th century B.C.
Votive
Preserved L: 26.9 cm; H: 3.2 cm; depth: 4 cm
Samos, Vathy Museum H 89

Göttlicher, 1978:65, no. 346; Gray, 1974:G26, no. H 17, G58, G90; *Kopcke, 1967:145, 148, no. 52, pl. 83, 4.

Badly preserved hull section of wooden boat model (warship?). Bow, stern, and much of hull missing; all surfaces badly abraded. One end more or less pointed; a groove or channel runs from pointed end almost to end of blunted end. Kopcke viewed the groove as natural (not man-made) and considers this fragment to be the oldest Samian wooden model on the basis of the crudity of workmanship.

Arch. 10. Ship model from river shingle, Heraion of Samos.
Mid 7th century B.C.
Votive
Preserved L: 54.8 cm; B: 5 cm; depth: 6 cm; original L: ca. 57 cm (Ohly); preserved L:B ratio: 11:1
Present location unknown (Göttlicher: Athens?)

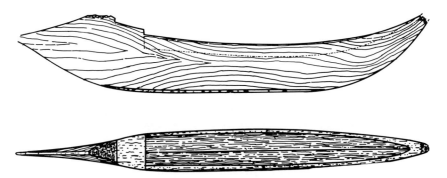

Arch. 10. Drawing by Vincent Amato, after Ohly, 1953.

Buschor, 1937:204; Casson, 1971:55, n. 71; Göttlicher, 1978:66, no. 352, pl. 26; Gray, 1974:G26, no. H 17, G58, G90, pl. XIIa; Kopcke, 1967:145; *Ohly, 1953:111–16, no. 25, 126, no. 25, figs. 27, 36, no. 25, pl. 34.

Well-preserved wooden warship model, carved from single block of wood. Tip of stern, top of bow compartment, and sections of starboard side and keel missing. Slender, attenuated proportions. Slightly rockered keel, which is rectangular in section, runs from bow to beginning of upcurving sternpost. In profile, stempost and sternpost rise equally steeply in a curve from the keel. Exaggeratedly large ram is incorporated into stempost and bow compartment; its pointed tip is at gunwale level. Long groove, triangular in section, runs longitudinally from abaft the bow compartment to the stern and represents the hull's undecked interior. It is probably triangular to provide support for the gunwales, which are flat along their upper surfaces. In section, hull at amidships is flat-bottomed, tapering to a deep-V configuration at bow and stern. Hull sides are straight and vertical amidships, convex toward either end. Flat foredeck slopes downward toward stern, from bow compartment. The second largest and one of the best preserved of all the Heraion models, and the only example from a well-dated context in the mid seventh century B.C.[59]

Arch. 11. Ship model from Heraion of Samos.
Mid 7th century B.C.
Votive
Preserved L: 19.6 cm; B: ca. 2.1 cm; preserved L:B ratio: 9.3:1
Present location unknown

Casson, 1971:55, nn. 71, 72; Göttlicher, 1978:66, no. 353, pl. 26; Gray, 1974:G26, no. H 17, G58, G90; Kopcke, 1967:145; *Ohly, 1953: 111–16, no. 26, 126, no. 26, figs. 28, 33, no. 26.

Well-preserved wooden warship model, carved from single block of wood. Tip of stern missing. Slender, attenuated proportions. Keel is flat for approximately one-third of total length; sternpost curves upward gradually; stempost meets keel at low angle. Tip of ram terminates midway between keel and deck level. Poop deck and bow compartment offset from deck level by one and two steps, respectively. Bow compartment flattened at top rather than pointed. Thwartships hole, just aft of amidships, midway between keel and deck level, may be either man-made or knot or root hole. Hull's greatest beam is just forward of amidships. In section, hull is flat-bottomed, hull sides slightly concave. In plan, gunwales are disproportionately thick; undecked hull interior is demarcated by groove (triangular in section) running between poop deck and bow compartment.

Arch. 12. Ship model from Heraion of Samos.

Mid 7th century B.C.

Votive

Preserved L: 40.4 cm; B: 2.5 cm; depth: 5 cm; preserved L:B ratio: 16.2:1; original L: ca. 50 cm (Ohly)

Present location unknown

Casson, 1971:55, nn. 71, 72; Göttlicher, 1978:66, no. 354, pl. 26; Gray, 1974:G26, no. H 17, G58, G90; Kopcke, 1967:145; *Ohly, 1953:111–16, no. 27, 126, no. 27, figs. 29, 36, no. 27.

Wooden warship model carved from single piece of wood. Tip of ram and bow compartment, section of hull at stern and amidships, and stern missing. Extremely slender, attenuated proportions. Flat keel rises in gentle curve at bow and stern. Projected height of ram tip is closer to deck level than level of keel. Top of bow compartment is rounded; deck is flat, rising in curve to bow and stern. In section, boat bottom is flat; hull sides are high and straight. Originally one of the largest models from the Heraion.

Arch. 13. Ship model from Heraion of Samos.

Mid 7th century B.C.

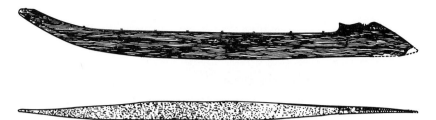

Arch. 13. Drawing by Vincent Amato, after Ohly, 1953.

Votive

Preserved L: 51.9 cm; B: 2.5 cm; H: 6.5 cm; preserved L:B ratio: 20.8:1

Present location unknown

Casson, 1971:55, n. 71; Göttlicher, 1978:66, no. 355, pl. 26; Gray, 1974:G26, no. H 17, G58, G90; Kopcke, 1967:145; *Ohly, 1953:111– 18, no. 28, 126, no. 28, figs. 30, 36, no. 28, pl. 35.

Wooden warship model carved from single block of wood. Tip of ram, nearby keel section, and top of bow compartment missing. Most extreme proportions of all the Heraion models (20.8:1). Keel slightly rockered, curving upward to stern. Projected tip of ram is close to level of keel. Deck is flat, with nine opposed pairs of wooden pins or dowels distributed at even intervals along outside edge of deck. These represent either tholepins or dowels for attachment of rails, gunwales, or spray screens. If the last named, the extreme proportions would be considerably reduced to closer to those of the other Heraion models. After edge of bow compartment curves up- ward and inward toward stern, offsetting it from deck. In section, hull at amidships is a deep-V configuration with slightly concave sides to waterline; above, hull sides are straight and vertical. Water- line marked by slight longitudinal bulge in hull side running from ram to stern. One of largest Heraion models.

Arch. 14. Boat model from Heraion of Samos.

Mid 7th century B.C.

Votive

Preserved L: ca. 50 cm; H: 7.3 cm

Present location unknown

Kopcke, 1967:145; *Ohly, 1953:111–18, no. 29, 126, no. 29, figs. 31–33, 36, no. 29, pl. 32 top.

Arch. 14. Drawing by Vincent Amato, after Ohly, 1953.

Built wooden model of merchant vessel, of which major portion of one side is preserved in several fragments. Short section of keel also is preserved; remainder missing. Low, elongated proportions, with strongly rockered keel. Angles of stem and stern are approximately equal, rising in gradual curve from keel to gunwale. In section, hull is of deep-V configuration, with slightly convex sides. Preserved keel section is pegged at regular intervals to hull by means of round wooden dowels set at slightly sloping angle to bottom of keel. Keel is rectangular in section like Arch. 10; its basal surface is set flush to bottom of hull. Small rectangular and circular holes in side of hull, in no discernible pattern, may have originally served as points to which thwarts, benches, and associated rigging were attached. The only built model from the ancient world.

Arch. 15. Ship model from area 014a–b (square 40/31), Heraion of Samos.
650–600 B.C.
Votive
Preserved L: 31.8 cm; B: 4.4 cm; preserved L:B ratio: 7.2:1
Samos, Vathy Museum H 90
*Kyrieleis, 1980:89–94, no. 1, fig. 1.1, pl. 18, 1–2.

Model of warship, carved from single block of wood. Tip of ram, section of gunwale and stern, and small section of bottom missing. Long, slender proportions. Keel slightly rockered, rising at stempost and sternpost in gradual curve. Ram tip almost at deck level. In section, both interior and exterior of hull are rounded, giving appearance of undecked vessel. High bow compartment.

Arch. 16. Ship model from area 014b (square 24), Heraion of Samos.
650–600 B.C.
Votive
Preserved L: 33.5 cm; B: 5.8 cm; preserved L:B ratio: 5.8:1
Samos, Vathy Museum H 91
*Kyrieleis, 1980:89–94, no. 2, fig. 1.3, pl. 18, 3.

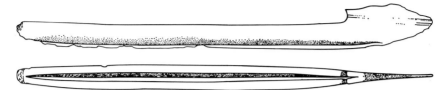

Arch. 17. Drawing by Vincent Amato, after Kyrieleis, 1980.

Model of decked (?) warship in two pieces, carved from single block of wood. Tip of ram and stern missing; surfaces worn. Long, slender proportions. Keel is flat, rising in sharp curve at stern, gradual curve at bow. Deck is flat, rising gradually at bow and stern. In section, hull sides are slightly convex amidships.

Arch. 17. Ship model from area 014b (square 24), Heraion of Samos. 650–600 B.C.
Votive
Preserved L: 62.5 cm; B: 3.5 cm; preserved L:B ratio: 17.9:1
Samos, Vathy Museum H 92

*Kyrieleis, 1980:89–94, no. 3, fig. 2.1, pl. 20, 1–2.

Model of undecked warship, carved from single block of wood. Stern, section of hull at stern, and top of bow compartment missing. All surfaces and edges worn. Long, very attenuated proportions. In profile, keel is flat. Keel is articulated at base of hull and is rounded in section. At section amidships, hull sides are convex. Preserved portion of trailing edge of bow compartment curves upward and aft toward stern. Long groove, triangular in section, runs from trailing edge of bow compartment to end of preserved portion of stern, indicating that ship is undecked. Largest of models from Heraion.

Arch. 18. Ship model from area 014b (square 44), Heraion of Samos. 650–600 B.C.
Votive
Preserved L: 39.7 cm; B: 3.3 cm
Samos, Vathy Museum H 93

*Kyrieleis, 1980:89–94, no. 4, fig. 2.3, pl. 19, 4.

Model of decked warship, carved from single block of wood. In two fragments. Tip of ram, entire bow compartment, top of stern missing; keel is chipped; entire surface badly worn. Slender, attenuated proportions. Keel is slightly rockered, rising in shallow curve at stem and steeper curve at stern. Vessel is triangular at amidships section, with slightly convex sides. Deck is flat, rising gradually at stem and stern.

Arch. 19. Ship model from area 014b (square 2), Heraion of Samos. 650–600 B.C.

Votive

Preserved L: 37.5 cm; B: 2 cm

Samos, Vathy Museum H 94

*Kyrieleis, 1980:89–94, no. 5, fig. 2.2, pl. 19, 5.

Model of decked warship, carved from single block of wood. In three fragments. Tip of ram, top of bow compartment, top of stern missing; keel at stern chipped; surface badly abraded. Knotholes at stern and amidships. Long, slender proportions. Flat bottom rises in gradual curve at stem and stern. Tip (missing) of ram almost at deck level. Flat deck rises in low curve to bow and stern. In section, hull is rectangular at amidships, with straight sides.

Arch. 20. Ship model from area 014b (square 41), Heraion of Samos. 650–600 B.C.

Votive

Preserved L: 37.3 cm; B: 2.7 cm

Samos, Vathy Museum H 95

*Kyrieleis, 1980:89–94, no. 6, fig. 1.2, pl. 19, 6.

Model of decked warship, carved from single block of wood. In three fragments. Tip of sternpost missing; all surfaces abraded. Slender, attenuated proportions. Keel is slightly rockered, rising in low curve at stem and stern. Deck and ship bottom are both flat. Bow compartment is triangular in section. Hull has straight sides to waterline, angling inward to flat bottom.

Arch. 21. Ship model from area 014b (square 12), Heraion of Samos. 650–600 B.C.

Votive

Preserved L: 35 cm; B: 2 cm; preserved L:B ratio: 17.5:1
Samos, Vathy Museum H 96

*Kyrieleis, 1980:89–94, no. 7, fig. 1.4, pl. 19, 2.

Model of decked warship, carved from single block of wood. In two fragments. Tip of ram, top of bow compartment, lower hull section forward of amidships, and top of stern missing. Low, attenuated proportions. Preserved portion of keel is slightly rockered, rising in gradual curve to stem and stern. Flat deck rises in gradual curve at bow and stern. In section, convex hull sides are slightly rounded.

Arch. 22. Ship model from area 013d (square 91), Heraion of Samos.
650–600 B.C.

Votive

Preserved L: 29.8 cm; preserved B: 2.8 cm

Samos, Vathy Museum H 97

*Kyrieleis, 1980:89–94, no. 8, pl. 19, 3.

Model of decked warship, carved from single block of wood. In two fragments. Ram, stern, lower midsection of hull missing; all surfaces badly worn. Long, slender proportions. Preserved portion of keel is rockered. Tip (missing) of ram is almost at deck level.

Arch. 23. Ship model from Heraion of Samos.
650–600 B.C.

Votive

Preserved L: 8 cm; preserved H: 3 cm

Samos, Vathy Museum H 98

*Kyrieleis, 1980:90–94, no. 9, pl. 19, 1.

Fragmentary warship model, of wood. Ram and forward end of bow preserved; remainder missing. Surface worn. Ram is pointed; preserved portion of keel indicates that bottom was originally slightly rockered.

Arch. 24. Ship model from Heraion of Samos.
650–600 B.C.

Votive

Preserved L: 21.5 cm; preserved B: 4.5 cm

Samos, Vathy Museum H 99

*Kyrieleis, 1980:90–94, no. 10, fig. 2.4.

Fragmentary wooden ship model. Bow, stern, and unknown portion of hull missing; preserved surfaces are worn. Fragment comprises section of hull; in section, the hull has straight sides to the waterline, below which is a concave taper to the rounded bottom. Preserved portion of bottom appears to be rockered.

Arch. 25. Boat model from North Dump, Potters' Quarter, Corinth. 650–625 B.C.

Function unknown

Preserved L: 4.6 cm

Corinth, Corinth Museum KT52-1

*A. N. Stillwell, 1952:195–97, no. 1, pl. 43.XXXI, 1.

Fragment of small craft model, of hard yellow clay. Low, beamy proportions, with what appear to be frames painted on interior and exterior in hard, orange-brown paint. Four frames painted on interior, of which two are diagonally oriented and two are properly thwartships. Boat bottom is rounded, with no indication of a keel. Fragment is "probably from bow" (A. N. Stillwell).

Arch. 26–28. Three boat models from votive deposit, quarter mile from border of Acropolis and Necropolis, Ischia (Pithecusae, Italy). 635–620 B.C.

Votives

Dimensions unknown

Superintendency storerooms, Lacco Ameno d'Ischia (temporarily)

Unpublished. Mentioned by Buchner, 1967:131, no. 1949; Morrison and Williams, 1968:84; D. Ridgeway, personal communication, 31 October 1980; Trendall, 1966–67:31.

Three boat models of "coarse pottery (impasto)—which one tends to assume . . . is local . . . heavily burnt . . . traces of paint survive . . . the external appearance of these boats is 'not unlike' that of the 7th century Corinthian example illustrated by Lucien Basch in *JHS* 97 (1977) pl. II, b–c; inside, ours have two or three seats indicated by rolled strips of clay"[60] ". . . with interesting details of stern fittings similar to those of the ship to the right on the Aristonothos krater."[61]

Arch. 29. Boat model from Corinth.
625–600 B.C.
Function unknown
Preserved L: 4.6 cm
Corinth, Corinth Museum KT52-2

Lloyd, 1975:53, n. 64; *A. N. Stillwell, 1952:195–97, no. 2, pl. 43. XXXI, 2.

Fragment of warship model of hard yellow clay, with added details in purple paint. Stern and short section of hull preserved; remainder missing. Low proportions, with hull sides almost vertical. Ship is flat-bottomed and undecked. Stern is decorated with goose or swan head, abraded on uppermost surface. Gunwale or cap rail delineated by applied strip of clay; additional thwartships strip near stern represents either bench, structural thwart, or possibly the lower half of a crew member (helmsman?). Hull's exterior, stern decoration, rear of thwart, and interior frames are marked by paint. For comparison, see Arch. 48.

Arch. 30. Spouted vessel in the form of a warship from Boeotia (?).
Geometric (Vermeule, Chase, C. H. Smith, Fairbanks)
Archaic (A. N. Stillwell)
7th century B.C. (Basch, Gray)
650–600 B.C. (Morrison and Williams)
Ca. 600 B.C. (Göttlicher)
Function unknown
L: 30 cm; B: 9.4 cm; H. 15 cm; L:B ratio: 3.2:1
Boston, Museum of Fine Arts 99.915

Basch, 1973:70, n. 25; Chase, 1950:12–14, fig. 10; Editors, *AA* 15 (1900): 219, no. 13; Fairbanks, 1928:83, no. 277, pl. XXIV; Göttlicher, 1978:66, no. 351, pl. 26; Gray, 1974:G26, no. H 15; *Kirk, 1951:339–43, pl. 34; Morrison and Williams, 1968:82, Arch. 30, pl. 10c; Robinson, 1899:56–57; C. H. Smith, 1899:no. 264; A. N. Stillwell, 1952:196, n. 13; Vermeule, 1963:28, pl. 21.

Arch. 30. Courtesy of the Museum of Fine Arts, Boston.

Drinking vessel or rhyton of "pinkish-brown clay, slightly glazed,"[62] in the form of a warship on three legs. Details in blackish-brown paint. Top of stempost and interior thwart in bow compartment missing; top of pouring spout slightly abraded. Bottom is deep and rounded in section; keel is strongly rockered, stempost and sternpost rising in steep curve from keel. Tip of ram is squared off as on Arch. 32, also from Boeotia. Tip of ram is at deck level and is decorated near the base with an oculus to either side. Vertical painted line separates ram from body of vessel. Waterline is marked by two horizontal lines between which alternate dots and reverse sigmas; latter may represent stylized waves. Bow compartment subdivided into small rectangles by three horizontal and ten vertical lines, depicting stanchions and rails. Stub of stempost is canted, with horizontal painted lines from base to break. Bow compartment interior has remains of an applied fixture; either a crewman (Kirk), a cathead (Morrison and Williams), or a thwart. Portions of an applied painted clay strip are visible on bow compartment exterior on starboard side. Deck slopes downward from either side of a longitudinal axial raised ridge and is decorated at the approximate midpoint by the filling spout. Spout decorated at the rim by a black line and at the shoulder by a circle of dots. Deck also has reversed sigmas along edges. At high stern, between two rails decorated with vertical lines, is a bearded crewman, painted black except for his face and neck. He is seated or semireclining on a thwart and is probably to be identified as the helmsman. Rounded pouring or drinking spout is incorporated into the sternpost. Best argument for the date of this model is made by Morrison and Williams, 1968:82, modifying Kirk, 1951.

Arch. 31. Boat model from destruction debris (associated with enlargement of Apollo Sanctuary) over house, Temple Hill, Corinth.
Before 580/70 B.C.

Votive

Preserved L: 6.4 cm, preserved H: 2.7 cm

Corinth, Corinth Museum MF-78-57

Unpublished. H. S. Robinson, personal communication, 18 February 1980, 31 March 1980.

Fragmentary small craft model of hard buff clay. One end and hull section preserved, badly abraded; remainder missing. Details in dull red paint. Low, broad proportions. Gunwale marked by red paint. Frames painted on interior and exterior, in both places intersecting a longitudinal axial line representing the keel. In profile, stempost or sternpost is vertically flattened, meeting keel at right angle. Preserved portion may be bow or stern, although the latter seems likelier.

Arch. 32. Kantharos or kyathos with warship attributes from Boeotia.
575–550 B.C.

Function unknown (secondary)

H: 17 cm; B: 27 cm

Paris, Louvre CA 577 (acquired 1893)

Beazley, 1956:30, no. 13; Charbonneaux et al., 1971:69–70, 402, fig. 75 (color); Couve, 1897:452–53, fig. 7; Kilinski, 1978:181–82, 191, figs. 14–15; Perrot and Chipiez, 1914 (vol. X):39–40, fig. 27; Pfuhl, 1923:129; Ure, 1927:12; *Waiblinger, 1974:27–28, pl. 22, 3–4; Weicker, 1902:147, fig. 71.

One-handled kantharos (or kyathos) of very pale brown clay, with details in red and white paint. Rim fragment near handle missing. Minor restorations in paint. Made at or near Tanagra, decorated by the Painter of Boston 01.8110.[63] Opposite handle, where other handle should be, is a warship prow, including squared-off boar's head ram (like Arch. 30) with painted mouth, tusk, cheek, eye, and brow. Above and abaft ram is a low bow compartment with vertical painted lines representing stanchions. Compartment is capped by slightly sheered stempost, painted solid brown. Handle opposite ram, which also serves to represent a curved sternpost, is topped by a finial decorated on either side by an oculus; small spur off handle

Arch. 32. Courtesy of the Louvre, Paris.

base may represent steering oar. Neck of cup is decorated with additional maritime motifs: to port (from left to right), a pair of leaping
dolphins, a Triton holding a grapevine in one hand and a fish in the
other, and a leaping dolphin. On the other side, a pair of leaping
dolphins, a cross motif, and a pair of winged facing sirens. Beneath
handle, a pair of lotus blossoms and a palmette motif vertically arranged, which vaguely recall the stern of Arch. 30. Kilinski connects
this vase and its maritime attributes with the Tanagran cult of Dionysos, citing Pausanius (9.20.4).[64]

Arch. 33. Boat model from Corinth.
Archaic (6th century B.C.?)
Function unknown
Preserved H: 3.8 cm; preserved B: 4.2 cm
Corinth, Corinth Museum KT52-4
*A. N. Stillwell, 1952:195–97, no. 3, pl. 43.XXXI, 3.

Stern and portion of hull of warship model of pale yellow clay.
Details in black and purple paint. Sternpost curves upward above
gunwale and recurves back into hull. Single frame painted on interior.
Most of hull's exterior is painted black, possibly to represent hull
sheathing. Horizontal purple stripe covers black stern on either side.

Arch. 34. Boat model from Corinth.
Archaic (7th–6th centuries B.C.)
Function unknown
Preserved L: 4.5 cm
Corinth, Corinth Museum KT52-3

*A. N. Stillwell, 1952:195, 197, pl. 43.XXXI, 4.

Bow and small hull section of warship model of light buff clay, with details in black paint. Wide proportions. Longitudinal ridge along bottom of exterior represents keel. Theriomorphic ram, set low, has mouth, nose, eye, and brow painted on end. Eyes are elliptical with dot irises; brows are arched and hooked at ends.

Arch. 35. Boat model from Corinth.
Archaic (7th–6th centuries B.C.)
Function unknown
Preserved L: 7.2 cm; preserved H: 2.7 cm
Corinth, Corinth Museum KT52-9
*A. N. Stillwell, 1952:195, 197, pl. 43.XXXI, 6.

Crudely fashioned warship model of hard, light brown clay. Tip of ram and forward edge of stempost missing. Low, heavy proportions. Flat bottom, with ram projecting forward directly from bottom surface. Sternpost curves upward, projecting slightly above gunwale to form the *aplustre*, or stern ornament. Rough, abraded surface is covered with artisan's fingerprints.

Arch. 36–44. Boat models from Corinth.
6th century B.C. (or possibly 7th century)
Functions unknown
Dimensions unknown
Corinth, Corinth Museum KT52-6 through KT52-15 (excluding KT52-9, which is Arch. 23)
Unpublished. Mentioned by A. N. Stillwell, 1952:195–97.

Presumably clay watercraft models or fragments. Stem of KT52-10 is "finished merely by pinching it into a point" (A. N. Stillwell).

Arch. 45. Boat model from large circular pit outside temple precinct, Isthmia.
6th century B.C.
Votive
L: 6.1 cm
Isthmia, Isthmia Museum IM 2429

*Broneer, 1959:301–3, 338, no. 6, pl. 73c; Göttlicher, 1978:65, no. 349.

Terracotta small craft model with details in dark paint. Tip of stern missing; surfaces abraded. Keel slightly rockered; stem- and sternposts are perpendicular to keel. Vertical painted line at bow represents stempost. Large amorphous blob of paint at bow depicts oculus. Gunwales indicated by painted lines, as are ten frames and keel on interior.

Arch. 46. Boat model from large circular pit outside temple precinct, Isthmia.

6th century B.C.

Votive

L: 9.3 cm; B: 2.8 cm; L:B ratio: 3.3:1

Isthmia, Isthmia Museum IM 2090

*Broneer, 1959:328, no. 8, fig. 5; Göttlicher, 1978:65–66, no. 350, pl. 26.

Bronze small craft model; chips missing from starboard gunwale and extremities of crew members. Surface corroded. Rounded proportions, stern and bottom. Prow ends in animal protome (deer?) much like the Sardinian models. Four crewmen inside, badly preserved. At prow is man facing aft, with arms crossed over chest. In center are two rowers side by side facing aft, with hands on oars. Oars extend over gunwales and down along hull's exterior. In stern,

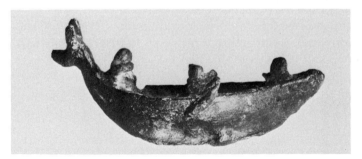

Arch. 46. Courtesy of the American School of Classical Studies, Athens, Greece.

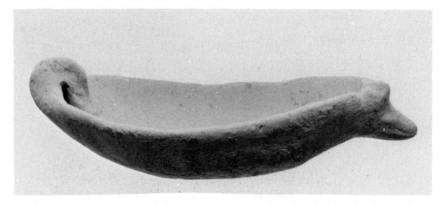

Arch. 47. Courtesy of the American School of Classical Studies, Corinth Excavations, Athens, Greece.

member of crew faces forward, with left arm over chest and right arm up, ostensibly gesturing.

Arch. 47. Boat model from Aphrodite Deposit, Potters' Quarter, Corinth.
Late 6th–early 5th centuries B.C.
Votive
L: 9.3 cm; B: 4.1 cm
Corinth, Corinth Museum KT52-5

Newhall, 1931:24, pl. I, right center; *A. N. Stillwell, 1952:196–97, pl. 43.XXXI, 5.

Clay model of undecked warship, hand-modeled of pinkish-buff clay. Chip missing from gunwale at bow. Short, very broad proportions, with strongly rockered keel. Sternpost curves upward above gunwale, then back down over interior. Ram projects from near gunwale level and inclines downward.

Arch. 48. Boat model from Corinth.
Late 6th century B.C.
Function unknown
L: 16.5 cm; H: 4.5 cm
London, British Museum 89.8-6.1 (purchased 1889)

Bass, 1972:58, fig. 15; Davies, 1978:85, n. 22; Göttlicher, 1978: 66, no. 356, pl. 26; *Higgins, 1954, vol. I, p. 245, no. 901, vol. II, pl.

Arch. 48. Courtesy of the Trustees of the British Museum, London.

130, no. 901; Lloyd, 1975:53, n. 63; Morrison and Williams, 1968:116, Arch. 100; A. N. Stillwell, 1952:196, n. 8; *Walters, 1903:76, no. B 36.

Model of undecked warship, of green clay. Details (ram, stempost, gunwales, stern decoration, occupants, and shields) in red paint. Low, beamy proportions. Proportionately oversized ram appears to emerge from boat bottom as straight extension of keel. Stempost rises high above gunwale level and is slightly canted aft. Sternpost curves upward above gunwale and doubles back over hull's interior. Gunwale is separately applied strip of painted clay. Five occupants, identified as armed marines (not crew) by shields on left arms. Three aftermost marines face forward; others face aft. Middle marine plays double flute and is perhaps to be identified as *auletes*. Presumably the vessel is shown en route to an engagement.

Arch. 49. Boat model from Sicily (possibly fake).
Late 6th–early 5th centuries B.C.
Function unknown
L: 52 cm; B: 17 cm; H: 19.5 cm (bow); L:B ratio: 3:1
Switzerland, private collection

Göttlicher, 1978:66–67, no. 356a, pl. 26; *Zimmerman, 1975:no. 200.

Intact terracotta small craft model; details in black and reddish-brown paint. Strongly rockered keel is articulated from bow to stern. Bow decorated with head of female wearing soft Phrygian cap; hair falls down to either side of head in two braids joined beneath chin.

Stern embellished with triangular fish tail,[65] decorated with alternating wide and narrow painted lines. Hull's exterior decorated with painted stylized waves, over which porpoises leap. Gunwale marked by thick black painted band with close-set incised vertical zigzag pattern. Each gunwale has three holes representing oarports evenly distributed along vessel's midsection. Three pairs of (removable) rowers sit side by side with arms up in front of their chests, a posture suggesting that they once held oars. In published photographs, however, the rowers sit backwards, facing forward. In the stern, a standing man with left arm missing and right arm to side. This figure, presumably the helmsman, is in a different scale and style from the other crewmen. The bizarre and unique admixture of decorative elements, the lack of specific provenience, and the differently scaled crew render the authenticity of this model suspect.

Arch. 50. Boat model from North Slope of Acropolis, Athens.
Archaic (?)
Votive
Preserved L: 7.1 cm; preserved B: 4.5 cm
Athens, Acropolis Museum (Göttlicher) or Agora Museum A-F 346

Göttlicher, personal communication; *Morgan, 1935:196–97, fig. 5h; A. N. Stillwell, 1952:196, n. 10.

Fragmentary bow of undecked warship model, of coarse reddish clay. Lower portion of hull and tip of ram preserved; surface badly abraded. Hull rounded on interior. Wide clay strip in interior near bow represents bench or thwart.

Arch. 51. Boat model from North Slope of Acropolis, Athens.
Archaic (?)
Votive
Preserved L: 6.2 cm; B: 3.2 cm
Athens, Acropolis Museum (Göttlicher) or Agora Museum A-F 393

Göttlicher, personal communication; *Morgan, 1935:196–97, fig. 5g; A. N. Stillwell, 1952:196, n. 10.

Model of undecked small craft of coarse reddish clay. One end and most of hull preserved. Low, shallow proportions. Keel, indicated by slightly raised ridge along bottom, is rockered. Preserved end (bow or stern?) is pointed. Interior of hull is triangular in section.

Arch. 52. Boat model from votive deposit, 2d–3d Hera Akraia Temple, Perachora.
Archaic
Votive
Preserved L: 6.2 cm
Athens, National Archaeological Museum (?)[66]

*Payne et al., 1940:97, pl. 29, no. 4; A. N. Stillwell, 1952:196, n. 10.

Model of undecked vessel of pale clay.[67] Tip of one end missing. Details in black paint. Low, wide proportions. Ends project upward to pointed terminals. Two transverse ridges in interior represent thwarts, benches, or possibly frames. According to Stillwell, Arch. 52 was manufactured across the Corinthian Gulf in the Potters' Quarter of Corinth.[68]

Arch. 53. Statue base in the form of a ship's prow (?), from vicinity of the Sanctuary of the Bulls, Delos.
End of the 7th century B.C. (Marcadé)
Archaic
Ca. 620–600 B.C. (Jeffery: inscription)
Votive statue base
L: 1.40 m; B: ca. 1.3 m (Göttlicher)
Delos, Delos Museum A728

Not fully published. Mentioned by Bruneau and Ducat, 1965:90, no. 24, 3; Couchoud and Svoronos, 1921:288–89, fig. 1; Göttlicher, 1978: 65, no. 348; Jeffery, 1961:291, 304, no. 3, pl. 55.3; Kern, 1913: pl. 6; Marcadé, 1946:151; Vallois, 1944:34, 287, fig. 3, 397–98; Walter-Karydi, 1980:3–4, pl. I, 3.

Stone statue base, either triangular, trapezoidal, or rectangular in plan.[69] Short end decorated with ram's head; on two other sides are gorgon masks. Inscribed on one side: "[Euthy- or Iphi-] cartides of Naxos." Graffito on one side depicts stern of unrigged ship. There is considerable confusion among the modern sources for this base, resulting from its incomplete publication. Most commonly, it is confused with the other trapezoidal base associated with the 246 B.C. dedication of the Sanctuary of the Bulls.

5

Classical Period

The major sources of information concerning seafaring in the Classical period are limited almost exclusively to literary and epigraphical references.[1] Considering the political, social, military, and economic importance of maritime activity during this period, the representational evidence for ships, water travel and transport, and naval warfare is scant.[2] The archaeological evidence is scarce too: only one shipwreck is known from the Classical period, dating to around 400 B.C.[3] To date, the relative paucity of nautical iconography in the Classical period has not been satisfactorily explained: Morrison and Williams have suggested rather unconvincingly that Classical ships were too complex to be accurately depicted and were thus avoided for the most part by contemporary artists and sculptors.[4]

Ship and boat models are especially rare during the Classical period. Of the four examples cataloged here and attributed to the period, none are securely dated and only two, Clas. 1 and 2, are from secure proveniences. Clas. 1 is from the Aeolic island of Lipari, off Sicily, and Clas. 2 is from the Erechtheion, on the Athenian Acropolis. The small number of examples and their insecure chronology preclude any worthwhile discussion of the geographical or temporal distribution of models for the period.

Architecture

With only one exception,[5] all of the ships and boats represented in any medium in the Classical period, including Clas. 1–4, are warships.[6] However, the presumption of Morrison and Williams that "a representation of an oared ship of complicated design coming from that [i.e., the Classical] period would depict a *trieres*"[7] is demonstrably invalid, since Clas. 2 and 3 are single-level ships, with auxiliary sails: perhaps third- or fourth-rate warships or courier or dispatch vessels, but certainly not *triereis*. Too little remains of Clas. 1 and 4 to positively identify their ship types, although the outriggers on Clas. 4 may indicate that it is a *trieres*, as will be discussed later.

Clas. 2 is one of the best preserved ship models from antiquity. Its only manifest architectural inaccuracy stems from a round lamp nozzle above and abaft the ram, which caused the sculptor to render the bow compartment somewhat smaller and farther aft than might normally be expected. Both bow and stern are partially decked; the stern is further marked by the presence to either side of a long, low railing supported near its forward end by a single stanchion, similar to those on Arch. 30 and on a number of other (painted) Archaic ship representations.[8] The rails continue around the sides of the stern-post and meet behind it. Along either gunwale, between the bow and stern decks, is a thick rope pattern, serving either as hull bindings (*hupozomata*)[9] or, as seems likelier in light of the length and height, as fenders.[10] The stern is decorated with a flattened incurved bifid terminal with a small incised oculus similar in placement to the oculus on Arch. 32. The hull's exterior is decorated just below the gunwale level with four incised lines which probably represent wales.[11] A number of compass-drawn circles between the wales and rope pattern (at least ten on the starboard side) clearly represent oarports. The keel of Clas. 2 is slightly rockered, terminating at its forward end in a thick blunted ram. In section, the sides of the hull are slightly convex, forming a deep-V configuration throughout the hull's length. At the hull's midpoint, the keel, rectangular in section, is articulated.[12] Toward the stern of the model, at the level of the incised wales, two rectangular excrescences protrude from the hull's exterior; from their position they appear to represent either the steering oar box[13] or possibly a thwartship timber supporting the stern deck. Two additional thwarts are present in the stern, and another is present in the bow at the after edge of the bow compartment. All are at gunwale level and appear from their placement to buttress the model's hull against buckling, and not to be structural ship's timbers. The vessel's interior is hollow between the thwarts, except for a large amorphous lump in the center, which may represent a mast stub.[14] Clas. 3 is similar to Clas. 2 in the treatment of the hollow hull, the lamp nozzle, the gunwale-level thwart, and the mast stub, and it is therefore attributed to the same general period.[15]

Clas. 1 and 4 are even more detailed than Clas. 2. However, the former is only a small fragment of a large model, while the latter is so extensively restored that it is difficult to determine which details are original and which are modern restorations.[16] Both Clas. 4 and the preserved portion of Clas. 1 depict prows of warships. On Clas. 1, a short section of the bow compartment and rail is preserved, the rail decorated with small circles (shields?) alternating with two or three vertical lines. Just below the bow compartment are a pair of wales separated by evenly alternating spaces and stanchions or exposed frames. These wales project from either side of the hull beyond the stempost and meet one another; the upper is blunted and the lower pointed. From their length and placement it seems possible that these wales may have served as subsidiary rams or as ram stops to prevent the ram from penetrating the enemy's hull too deeply. Clas. 4 has a similar wale and exposed stanchion (or frame) arrangement, although on it the vertical members are unevenly spaced. The oculus of Clas. 1 is below the wales, whereas the oculus on Clas. 4, in the form of the eye of a complete dolphin, is above the wales, in the area corresponding to the bow compartment.

Clas. 4 also has to either side the forward edge of an outrigger for an oar bank, which rests upon a solid diagonal strut butted against the lower wale. The presence of outriggers indicates that the ship after which Clas. 4 was patterned must have been a *trieres*, since on single- and double-banked warships in antiquity the oars were plied through oarports or over the gunwales or both, but not by means of outriggers.[17] The forward surface of each outrigger has a pair of small bossed circles horizontally disposed; these circles have been interpreted as subsidiary rams,[18] although they are probably set too far aft to have served this purpose.[19] It seems likelier that the artist either used the circles as a decorative motif to fill the available space or possibly misplaced the oarports, setting them along the *epotides* rather than along the side of the outrigger.[20]

Too little of Clas. 1 is preserved to ascertain its ship type. However, since like Clas. 4 it has a pair of horizontal wales separated by vertical members, its hull construction was probably similar to that of Clas. 4.

Functions

As has already been mentioned, only Clas. 1 and 2 of the four models attributed to the Classical period are from precise proveniences; the findspots for Clas. 3 and 4 are unknown. Furthermore, although both Clas. 1 and Clas. 2 are from votive contexts, it is unclear whether their use as votives was primary or secondary, since either model may previously have served another function.

Clas. 2 is the earliest manifestation of nautical iconography applied to a lamp. Unfortunately, its date, and consequently the date of this innovation, are disputed and may not at present be limited to a narrower range than the fifth or fourth centuries B.C.[21] The provenience and date of Clas. 3 are unknown as well and do not clarify the problem. However, the fact that Clas. 2 was cast in bronze may indicate that it was not a common lamp for everyday use; normally in Athens during the Classical period, lamps were small round spouted bowls of glazed clay with little decoration.[22] In light of its dedicatory inscription to Athena, it might be presumed that Clas. 2 was specifically manufactured as a votive, perhaps to be used in a religious procession to the Acropolis and there dedicated. Certainly, the custom had precedents, since nautical votives had been dedicated on the Acropolis in the Bronze Age (BA 22) and possibly in the Archaic period as well (Arch. 50 and 51). However, as Morrison and Williams have observed,[23] the inscription upon Clas. 2 appears from the letter forms to belong to the fourth century B.C. while the model itself more closely resembles the standard longship of the fifth or even the sixth century B.C.[24] From this chronological anomaly it might be inferred that Clas. 2 was manufactured as an expensive household object or souvenir in the Archaic or Classical periods and then inscribed and dedicated after the completion of the Erechtheion in 406 B.C. It is equally possible that Clas. 2 was originally dedicated at the old Athena temple beneath the Erechtheion, found during the latter's construction and inscribed as a dedication to Athena, and then rededicated at or near its original findspot. An alternative hypothesis is that the model and its inscription are both of the fourth century B.C. and that its archaistic form is the result of religious or architectural conservatism.

The origins of Clas. 4 may be sought in the Archaic period, when drinking or ritual rhytons in the form of ships are first identified (Arch. 1, 30, and 32). However, all of the Archaic rhytons incorporate complete ships, whereas Clas. 4 includes only the prow. Another possible source might therefore be certain late Archaic coins, such as those from Zankle (not far from Apulia, where Clas. 4 was manufactured), which have on their obverse warship prows, but not entire vessels.[25] A third alternative might be that Clas. 4 lacked an artistic prototype altogether and was an original rather than a derivative vase within the general context of Apulian plastic vases with marine iconography, which otherwise includes lobster claws, dolphins, seashells, frogs, and the like.[26]

CATALOG

Clas. 1. Ship model from bothros, Acropolis, Lipari.[27]
6th–5th centuries B.C.

Clas. 1. Courtesy of Dr. Nicholas B. Hartmann, by permission of the Museo Archeologico Eoliano, Lipari, Sicily.

Votive

Preserved L: 7 cm; preserved H: 5.1 cm

Lipari, Museo Archeologico Eoliano A15 (Room 10)

Unpublished.

Clay fragment of portside bow of molded warship model, with details in black, brown, and white paint. Interior rough and unpainted; finger marks visible. Bow compartment rail marked by circles (shields?) alternating with double painted lines. Below bow compartment are two thick horizontal wales, which extend from either side beyond the stempost and meet one another. Upper wale blunt at tip; lower wale pointed. Wales are separated by alternating spaces and timbers; timbers are either exposed stanchions, foredeck beams, or frames. Below wales is a large oculus with tear duct at top and large solid iris; eye is outlined in thin black paint. Preserved section of stempost is slightly sheered, tapering sharply from bottom to top. Tentatively attributed to the Classical period by the oversized eye and tear duct and wale structure, which closely resemble those of Clas. 4. Probably not originally a container for liquids, since interior is rough and unglazed.

Clas. 2. Lamp in form of warship, from hole in west transverse wall, central chamber, Erechtheion, Acropolis, Athens.

Clas. 2. Courtesy of the National Archaeological Museum, Athens, Greece.

Archaic–6th century B.C. (Basch)
5th century B.C. (Morrison and Williams)
4th–3d century B.C. (Göttlicher)
Votive
L: 30 cm; B: 7 cm; L:B ratio: 4.28:1
Athens, National Archaeological Museum 7038

Basch, 1969b:442–43, fig. 5A; 1972:44–45, pl. 30; 1975:210; Daremberg et al., 1912 (vol. 3):1325, fig. 4587; Göttlicher, 1978:68, no. 362, pl. 27; Kennedy, 1976:162; Lloyd, 1975:48, n. 25; Moll, 1929:BVIII, 1; Morrison and Williams, 1968:49, 178–79, Clas. 20, 292, pl. 27b; Paton, 1927:572, fig. 229; *Pittakes, 1862:91–94, with figure; *Rhousopoulos, 1862:39, no. 9; De Ridder, 1896:139–41, pl. 95; Stais, 1907:230–31, no. 7038, with figure.

Cast bronze model of single-level warship. Short section of keel missing amidships. Slightly rockered keel, articulated for most of vessel's length, is rectangular at amidships section. Thick ram with blunted tip extends directly from keel. Above and abaft ram is large rounded lamp nozzle. Behind nozzle is undersized bow compartment at level of gunwale. Abaft gunwale at same level is thick thwart, probably unconnected with ship architecture. Gunwale or cap rail along midsection of hull is marked by thick rope pattern, probably representing a bumper. Four incised lines below gunwale or cap rail, running from lamp nozzle base to stern deck represent pair of wales. Compass-drawn circles between rope pattern and wales (at least 11 on starboard side) probably represent oarports. Midway between keel and wales, in center of port side, is inscribed in stippled lettering:

ΙΕΡΟΝΤΗΣΑΘΗΝΑΣ

("a sacred thing for Athena"). Hull interior contains thickened bronze lump in center: probably mast stub or base for suspension hook. Proportionately oversized rail at stern is supported by thick vertical stanchion. From either side of hull, rails curve around and meet behind sternpost. Small deck in stern, with thick thwart just forward of its leading edge. Sternpost, flattened in plan, rises in steep curve from keel, and has bifid terminal with small engraved oculus. At stern, rectangular protuberances on hull's exterior represent structural thwart, cathead for stern landings, or steering oar box. In section, hull has deep-V configuration with slightly convex sides. Many details and overall form of this model are best paralleled by Archaic ship depictions, although inscription is dated by the letter forms to the fourth century B.C.[28]

Clas. 3. Lamp in form of warship model
14th century B.C. (Anonymous)
5th–4th centuries B.C.
Lamp (findspot unknown)
L: 15.2 cm; B: 2.7 cm; H: 3.8 cm; L:B ratio: 5.6:1
Cincinnati, Cincinnati Art Museum 1962.392 (W. T. and L. Taft Semple Collection, acquired in 1937 from George Karo, in Athens)

Anonymous, 1965, unpaginated, with photograph and caption; *Sculpture Collection of the Cincinnati Art Museum*, 1970, p. 34, no. 1962.392, with photograph.

Bronze model of undecked single-level warship. Portions of bow compartment and starboard side of hull missing. Keel slightly rockered. In profile, ram is short and rounded; in plan, it is sharp. Above ram is large rounded lamp nozzle with leading edge bent upward. After edge of nozzle is bridged by leading edge of bow compartment (the stempost?). Low bow screens are offset from gun-

Clas. 3. Courtesy of the Cincinnati Art Museum, the William T. and Louise Taft Semple Collection.

wale by low step. Thick, wide amidships thwart at gunwale level probably represents mast partner. Trailing edge of thwart butted by mast stub with slightly rounded top, preserved to above gunwale level. Aft of mast stub, gunwale is stepped upward, and is stepped upward again at stern. Sternpost curves upward steeply from keel. In section, hull has deep-V configuration, with straight sides. Similarity of lamp nozzle, bow compartment, mast stub, and deep-V hull to analogous features on Clas. 2 provides dating criteria.

Clas. 4. Drinking rhyton in form of warship prow.
Ca. 400 B.C. (Göttlicher)
4th century B.C. (Morrison)
Findspot unknown
L: 17.5 cm; H: 18.5 cm
Paris, Petit Palais 411

Göttlicher, 1978:67, no. 358, pl. 27; Morrison, in the work of Greenhill, 1976: 169, fig. 114; Morrison and Williams, 1968:178, Clas. 15, 280, pl. 26c; *Plaoutine, 1941:45–46, pl. 47, 1–3.

Rhyton in form of warship prow, of yellowish clay with reddish surface in places. Details in matt black, black glaze, yellow, and white paint. Restored portions include sides and lower part of ram, portions of wave pattern along base, scalloped edge of bow compartment and stempost, painted panels with floral patterns behind and above dolphins, lower palmette on back, neck, and both heads on neck. Above flat reserved bottom is a horizontal black glazed zone, with reserved band above and zone of wave pattern in black on reserved background above that. These three zones join to form the blunted ram. Tip of ram is subdivided into three sections by two vertical incised lines. Above and abaft ram are two wales separated by three unevenly spaced vertical timbers, representing either stanchions or frames as they do on Clas. 1. Lower wale projects farther forward than upper. Both wales have small dots painted on vertical surfaces, possibly depicting nails. Leading edge of stempost is scalloped in profile and is sheered aft to merge into bow compartment. Bow compartment is decorated with simple floral pattern. Small triangular space formed between wales and stempost is filled with schematized dolphin with oversized eye. Above dolphin, two diagonal lines follow line of sheered stempost. Outrigger for uppermost bank of oars is supported by a solid diagonal strut butted into lowermost wale. Strut is decorated with simple floral pattern. Forward edge of each outrigger is decorated between two horizontal lines with two small circles with

Clas. 4. Courtesy of the Ville de Paris, Musée du Petit Palais, Paris.

boss in center, possibly representing subsidiary rams,[29] shields, or covered oarports. Backs of outriggers decorated only with two horizontal lines. Vase handles spring upward from upper surfaces of outriggers. Neck of rhyton decorated with palmettes at handles with female head in front and male head behind, almost totally restored. Zone of dots below neck, and wave pattern at mouth. On back of rhyton, behind handles, are two superimposed palmettes. Presence of outriggers indicates that rhyton represents a *trieres*.

6

Hellenistic Period

As was true in the Archaic period, in the Hellenistic period the number of ship and boat models produced increased markedly; 39 examples, or nearly 10 times the number from the Classical period, have been found. This increase seems to have resulted not from an increase in seafaring activity, for which there is little evidence, but from the growing popularity of nautical imagery in contemporary art. In the Hellenistic period, ships and marine iconography appear for the first time in a variety of media, including mosaics and monumental sculpture, and they continue to be popular on coins and in wall paintings. Full and partial models of ships and boats are especially well represented from the beginning of the Hellenistic period.

Of the 39 Hellenistic models, 27 are from Greece. However, only one of these is from the Greek mainland (Hell. 4, from Epidauros); the others are from the Aegean islands of Delos (Hell. 11, 12, and 14–30), Rhenia (Hell. 9), Rhodes (Hell. 5 and 32), Kos (Hell. 13), Samothrace (Hell. 6), and Thasos (Hell. 8). Magna Graecia is represented by a single example (Hell. 3), and the rest of Italy by two of the earlier models for the period (Hell. 1 and 7). In addition, four examples are known from western Anatolia (Hell. 10, 33, 34, and 37), and for the first time, two from North Africa (Hell. 31) and Egypt (Hell. 36).[1] Four other examples tentatively attributed in the catalog to the Hellenistic period are from unknown proveniences (Hell. 2, 35, 38, and 39).

The more widespread geographical distribution of Hellenistic models away from mainland Greece toward the east (and to a lesser extent, the west as well) is probably a result of the overall spread of Hellenic culture initiated by Alexander the Great and continued by his generals and their descendants, who subdivided and administered his conquered lands. The clustering of models from Delos (and Rhenia) surely reflects Delos's primary activity as a free port from 166 to 69 B.C.

Architecture

None of the 39 Hellenistic models sufficiently well preserved to be classified depict small craft; moreover, only a single example (Hell. 3) is clearly not a warship. Hell. 3, with a length-to-beam ratio of 2.9:1, appears to represent a beamy, undecked merchant vessel with high, rounded ends and the point of maximum beam slightly forward of amidships. However, the architecture is ambiguous in that just below and slightly forward of the high, pointed stempost there is a short beak, which might be the modeler's attempt to depict a ram. Nonetheless, the short length of this feature and its position at gunwale level well above the waterline favor the interpretation that it is not a ram but a swelling formed by wales extending from either side around the stempost and meeting one another beyond it.

Since only the stern is depicted on Hell. 7, it is not possible to be certain whether a warship or merchant vessel was originally intended. However, if its features are compared with those of contemporary and later ship depictions, a warship seems more likely to have been intended. One of its most characteristic features is the slenderly proportioned stern, which in section has a deep-V configuration.[2] A merchant vessel might be expected to be somewhat broader in the stern in order to provide more cargo space. In addition, the pattern of alternating wales and strakes on Hell. 7 is best paralleled by contemporary and later warships, on which the presence of such a proportionately high number of wales would provide additional longitudinal strength for ramming tactics.[3] The small amount of surface area on the preserved portion of the steering oar blade might also indicate that Hell. 7 represents a warship, since the steering oars on merchant vessels normally had larger blades than did those on warships.[4]

One of the best preserved features of Hell. 7 is the steering oar housing, located on the port quarter (the roughly finished starboard side lacks this element). The housing appears to represent the aftermost end of the outrigger or oar box as well, since it is open at the leading edge. With simple moldings at the top and along the upper edge of the base, the housing is narrow in width and set close to the hull of the ship. The steering oar itself is set diagonally into the housing, abutting the hull, its upper end projecting above the top of the housing. Just below the rounded oar top is a groove perpendicular to the oar's longitudinal axis, which may have served as a lashing point for the tiller; the tiller, however, has become disconnected and is partially preserved in the hands of the helmsman at the end of the stern. The lower end and blade of the steering oar emerge from the lower aft corner of the housing. The arrangement of the oar and its housing is considerably less complex than that of the corresponding elements on the stern of the ship on a relief from Lindos of around 200 B.C.,[5] and in the absence of further evidence from the Hellenistic period, it more closely resembles the disposition of the steering oar on Roman ships from the first century B.C. through the second century A.C.[6] Just aft of the housing is a gunwale or rail supported by three slender stanchions; the bays between the two forwardmost stanchions are solidly filled, while the two after bays are open. The slender proportions and inverted-L form of the stanchions, which duplicate those on the Lindos relief, appear to indicate that the original architectural elements after which they were modeled were made of metal. Hell. 7 is one of only two models from the Hellenistic period with a crew; the crew figure presumably represents the helmsman or possibly Odysseus himself.[7]

Excluding Hell. 8, 16–25, 27, and 38, of which too little is preserved to determine their ship types, all of the remaining Hellenistic models are of warships. Hell. 1, one of the earliest, is also the most elaborately detailed, following in the tradition of Clas. 4. Like Clas. 4, it incorporates the bow of a warship into a two-handled rhyton with a flat base. In profile, its ram is formed by the superimposition of three knife or spear points which decorate the sides of three horizontal plates, themselves forming the striking surface of the ram proper.[8] A vertical strut, joining the three horizontal plates at their midpoint, terminates at its base in a small lion's-head spout.[9] The transformation of warship ram iconography from a boar's head to superimposed dagger blades seems to have begun early in the Hellenistic period;[10] Hell. 1 may be the earliest manifestation of this phenomenon. This new decoration continued to be popular throughout antiquity and could on occasion adopt the form of a trident as well, as it does on Hell. 31.[11] On Hell. 1 the tripartite ram forms the termination of a thickened wale that extends aft to the back of the rhyton. Above the ram wale are three more horizontal wales of which the leading ends extend from either side beyond the stempost and meet one another, in an arrangement similar to that of the wales on Clas. 4. Also like the latter, the lowermost pair of wales on Hell. 1 are separated by four thickened vertical lines alternating with spaces at uneven intervals, which appear to depict exposed stanchions or frames. On Hell. 1 these wales are composed of three timbers for the lowermost pair and two for the uppermost pair of wales. Although it seems unlikely, it is possible that the protruding wale ends may have served as *proembola*, or subsidiary rams.[12] The uppermost wale is short, extending aft only as far as the first vertical stanchion. Behind the wale, in the area corresponding to the bow screen, there is a dolphin in low relief, with an oversized beak and eye, very similar to the dolphin on Clas. 4.[13] Abaft the dolphin and resting upon the middle wale is a structure in the form of an inverted L, decorated with a female protome on its leading surface. By analogy with Clas. 4, this structure appears to represent the *epotis* of the oar box. If so, Hell. 1 would represent at least a two-banked warship, and probably a *trieres*. On top of the bow compartment is seated a female figure, possibly a Victory.[14] The remaining decoration on Hell. 1 is manifestly nonnautical.

One element of nautical iconography that first appears on ship models during the Hellenistic period is a small shield or boss decorating the *aphlaston*. This feature first appears on painted representations of Attic warships in the Geometric period,[15] and is also seen twice in the Archaic period: once on an Etruscan warship[16] and again on an Attic warship.[17] The shield or boss is not known to appear in the Classical period, but it reemerges in the Hellenistic period on the Lindos relief, ca. 200 B.C.[18] Its presence throughout antiquity only upon warships allows Hell. 16 and 17 to be identified with some certainty as fragments of warships rather than merchant vessels.

As has been mentioned previously, oars are rarely depicted upon Greek watercraft models, appearing only once in each of the Geometric and Archaic periods (Geom. 6 and Arch. 46). They appear in the Hellenistic period only on Hell. 29, 30, and 36. On Hell. 29 and 30, which are identical, the oars are represented by parallel incisions on the upper surface of the outrigger on either side of the vessel, bounding on each side three lamp nozzles. On Hell. 36, oar stubs are visible on either side of the vessel, arranged in three levels: the lowest level protrudes from the hull, the middle from between the middle deck stanchions, and the uppermost from between the upper deck stanchions. From this configuration, it is clear that Hell. 36 is one of the few identifiable examples of a *trieres* from the ancient world.

Hell. 29, 30, and a number of other Hellenistic models from Delos (Hell. 14, 15, 19, and 23–25) have thick heavy thwarts or benches at regular intervals spanning their interiors. In all cases these members abut a flat raised molding (possibly representing the gunwale) slightly higher than the thwarts. This raised molding runs completely around the hulls' interiors, separating the thwarts from external decorative zones filled with tongue, cord, or floral patterns. The spaces between the thwarts may either be solidly filled or contain filled, open, rounded, or lozenge-shaped motifs. On three of the models (Hell. 14, 24, and 25) the oval motif is open and may represent the filler holes for the lamps. It is unclear whether the spaces between the thwarts represent deck space when solid and hatches when filled with oval or lozenge-shaped elements, or whether these are simply decorative or functional lamp details. On those examples on which the lamp nozzles are preserved (Hell. 14, 15, 29, and 30), they are incorporated into the oar box, rather than the bow, where nozzles were located on models from the Classical period and on a single example tentatively dated to the Hellenistic period (Hell. 2). Excepting only the latter model, all of the Hellenistic lamps in the form of ships have multiple nozzles, unlike their Classical counterparts.

Hell. 35, of unknown provenience, is only tentatively attributed to the Hellenistic period. It includes a number of anomalous features otherwise unknown in ancient ship representations.[19] Chief among these anomalies is an upper deck running the length of the vessel which is supported by thick vertical stanchions, themselves probably extensions of the ship's frames.[20] In profile, the deck is curved, following the line of the rockered keel; it is pierced at its approximate midpoint by a hatch in the form of a D, of which the straight bar faces forward. Along the deck on the ship's port side is a wavy applied clay strip surmounted by another horizontal strip; together these two strips probably represent a railing or gunwale, possibly with oarports below.[21] However, if the wavy lines depict oarports, the manufacturer omitted rowers' benches at the level of the deck, since aside from the applied strips along the edge, the deck is featureless. Two thwarts are present in the vicinity of the bow. One is at deck level at the trailing edge of the bow compartment; whether it functions as a structural member or as a modeler's strut is uncertain. The other thwart, at gunwale level directly below the first thwart, may be a cathead,[22] the *epotis*, or possibly a deck support for the foredeck and bow compartment. A number of diagonal ridges in low relief along the hull beneath the gunwale may be hull bindings,[23] stylized waves,[24] or possibly vestigial oars.

Another characteristic feature of Hell. 35, aside from the unique high deck and its embellishment, is the deck support, which is in the form of broad vertical stanchions. They are paralleled by similar supports on painted representations from as early as the Geometric period and do not therefore represent diagnostic chronological criteria.[25] Hell. 36, from Egypt, also only tentatively attributed to the Hellenistic period, has similar deck stanchions,[26] as does another terracotta model ascribed to the Roman Republican period.[27] On Hell. 36, a *trieres* model, two upper decks are supported by vertical stanchions, which are probably extensions of the frames. However, the manufacturer erred in not placing the upper deck stanchions directly above the lower deck stanchions instead of staggering them. The tops of the stanchions are concealed behind a row of six shields attached to the deck rail on either side of the vessel, centered on the stanchions. On Hell. 36, there are only five oars on the lower bank, seven on the middle bank, and six on the upper bank, an indication that the modeler has greatly shortened the central hull section. On the other hand, that the long blunted ram and the steering oar to either side are greatly enlarged has led some scholars to dismiss the model altogether as valid evidence for ancient shipbuilding.[28] Basch has convincingly demonstrated that the combination of certain elements of Hell. 36 (the row of shields, the upper deck and stanchion configuration, the long ram, the convex stempost, the absence of outriggers and wales) indicates that the modeler's paradigm was probably a Phoenician *trieres* of the Hellenistic period.[29]

By the fourth century B.C., the presence of outriggers on ship representations no longer serves as a criterion for identifying a Greek *trieres*. During the fourth century, a number of new warship types were introduced into use by various navies around the Mediterranean and were used extensively until around 250 B.C.[30] Comparatively little is known of the specific arrangements of rowers and oar banks for these new vessels, on account of a dearth of identifiable representations of the individual types. Almost everything known of these vessels is derived from literary sources, most of which were written later than the period with which they were concerned.[31] However, it seems certain that irrespective of the number of oar banks, these new vessels had outriggers and were manned by more than a single man per oar, unlike the *trieres*.[32]

Two of the least known warship categories first mentioned in relation to the fourth century B.C. are the *hemiolia*, of which little is known, and the *trihemiolia*. The *trihemiolia* is first and most usually associated with the island of Rhodes, beginning around 304 B.C.[33] From its lengthy inscription devoted to a crew's list of a group of *trihemioliai*, it may be presumed that Hell. 5, from Rhodes, is one of the few identifiable representations of the *trihemiolia* warship type.[34] It comprises the badly preserved remains of the prow of a warship floating over schematized waves, the whole composed of four courses of local marble.[35] The lowermost course comprises the base with waves and the lower hull section of the ship proper. Nothing is preserved of the ram or stempost. The second course has along its lower edge a rectilinear fillet representing a thickened wale; its upper section reverts to undifferentiated hull strakes. The third course is devoted to the outrigger, which springs outward sharply from the hull. In section, the profile of the lower surface of the outrigger is concave rather than straight (as on Clas. 4) or horizontal (as on Hell. 1). Unlike the corresponding elements on Clas. 4 and Hell. 1 and 11, the *epotis* of Hell. 5 is slanted diagonally aft; its upper and lower surfaces are bordered with a decorative fillet. The fourth course, representing the bow compartment, also has a fillet around its upper edge.

Hell. 6, also of Rhodian marble,[36] is architecturally similar to Hell. 5. Like Hell. 5, it has undifferentiated strakes separated by a rectangular wale, outriggers with oblique *epotides* and concave undersurfaces, and decorative moldings on the upper and lower outrigger edges. While Hell. 5 has a single molding at the upper edge of the bow compartment, Hell. 6 has two, of which the upper example merges into the stempost.[37] Enough of the stempost of Hell. 6 is preserved to verify that it is essentially vertical, although how it merged with the ram is unknown, since the ram is not preserved.[38] Most of the differences between Hell. 5 and 6 are found on the outrigger, which is more detailed on Hell. 6. The *epotides* on Hell. 6 extend beyond the outer longitudinal edge of the outrigger, perhaps to protect and strengthen the joint between the two elements; on Hell. 5 the moldings carry around the *epotis* directly onto the body of the outrigger without a break. Additionally, on Hell. 6 the vertical outrigger surface is provided with two vertically staggered oarports, which are lacking on Hell. 5. The presence of two oarports at two levels presumably indicates that two banks of oars could be plied through the outrigger of a Hellenistic warship, whereas a single bank was plied through the outrigger of a *trieres* of the Classical period. The ports on Hell. 6 adopt the form of an oblong in low relief, with a vertical tholepin bisecting the opening; a similar oarport without the tholepin appears partially preserved on Hell. 31.[39] Other embellishments on Hell. 6 not present on Hell. 5 include more complex moldings at various places and a quarter-round strut at the after end of the oar box. This strut is presumably sculptural rather than architectural, since it is otherwise unknown in ancient nautical iconography. The similarities between Hell. 5 and 6 have led some scholars to attribute the latter to the *trihemiolia* class of warship,[40] although in the absence of more specific iconographical or literary evidence it is not possible to be certain.[41]

The remaining Hellenistic models are either too fragmentary or too schematic to be of much architectural interest.

Functions

As is the case in earlier periods, in the Hellenistic period there are both continuity of function and new applications for ship and boat models. Thus, for example, Hell. 1 continues the tradition set as early as the Archaic period (Arch. 1, 30, and 32) and continued during the Classical period (Clas. 4) of producing rhytons in the form of ship's prows. It also terminates that tradition, for it is the last vase in that form in Greek (and Roman) antiquity.

Lamps in the form of warships are also well represented in the Hellenistic period. Hell. 2, of unknown provenience and date, has a single lamp nozzle at the bow, as do Clas. 2 and 3, although neither the form of the nozzle nor that of the ship itself conforms to the Classical paradigm. Hell. 14–30 are also all lamps in the form of warships, but they have multiple nozzles along their sides and only occasionally a single nozzle at the bow (Hell. 14, 15, 29, and 30).[42] All were found at various places around the island of Delos; their manifest uniformity of form suggests that they were all manufactured at or around the same time, presumably between 166 and 69 B.C., when Delos was a thriving free port.[43] As P. Bruneau has stated in his publication of the Delian lamps,[44] none of the ship-shaped lamps with specific proveniences were found in votive or funerary contexts.[45] Rather, they were found either in public places (Hell. 15, 20, 27, and 29) or in domestic contexts (Hell. 14 and 22), which would appear to suggest ex silentio that they fulfilled utilitarian and not ritual purposes. If so, their form ostensibly reflects a generalized contemporary interest in maritime affairs applied to ordinary objects. A similar hypothesis might also explain why the earliest sundial from the gymnasium of Delos took the form of a warship prow (Hell. 11).[46] Alternately, all of these ship-shaped but otherwise utilitarian objects might be generic souvenirs of what must have been one of the most elaborate and bizarre nautical votives from antiquity: the ship in the Sanctuary of the Bulls on Delos.[47]

Several miniature lead and bronze anchors have also been found on Delos, in an area north of the Agora of Theophrastus, and on Rhenia, in an unspecified number of graves. Deonna considered the Delian anchors to be toys or ex-votos and the Rhenian examples to be souvenirs of the decedent's profession or possibly symbolic images of hope or good luck.[48] Similarly, Hell. 9, a marble ship's prow that orginally embellished a funerary monument in the necropolis on Rhenia, may have either celebrated the decedent's profession or symbolized the formal departure of the dead from the land of the living: a number of grave stelae with ship iconography from Rhenia do involve scenes of leave-taking.[49] Similar motives might explain the manufacture of Hell. 12, a marble funerary altar with a warship prow from Rhodes.

In the Hellenistic period, three-dimensional ship iconography appears for the first time as an integral element of monumental sculpture. Its earliest manifestation may be Hell. 4, a statue base in the form of a schematized warship prow floating over the waves, from the southeast corner of Building K (a bath building of the Classical period) just outside the perimeter of the Asklepion at Epidauros. Hell. 4 has been dated to the late fourth century B.C. on the basis of the letter forms of its dedicatory inscription, which includes the names of the dedicants and artist.[50] The base originally held a small statue of an unknown sort; some modern scholars have suggested that it held a Victory figure.[51] Together, the base and crowning statue were erected before, but not aligned with, a small exedra at the corner of the bath building nearest to the large open space before the temple to Asklepios, outside the temenos proper.[52] The dedicatory inscription, which includes the phrase

ΑΠΟΤΩΝΠΟΛΕΜΙΩΝ

("from the enemy") suggests that the dedication to "[all ?] the gods" commemorated a battle victory, presumably naval on account of the nautical iconography. No other information concerning the battle is provided by the original inscription. The presence of a later inscription by the Roman consul L. Mummius, sacker of Corinth in 146 B.C., indicates that the base was still conspicuously situated in the mid second century B.C. and possibly still associated with victory.[53] The motives behind the placement of Hell. 4 at the Asklepion of Epidauros are unclear, since the Greeks did not particularly associate Asklepios with seafaring.[54]

The next earliest manifestation of monumental nautical sculpture is Hell. 5, erected against the back wall of the east wing of the stoa at the sanctuary of Athena at Lindos, Rhodes, around 265–260 B.C.[55] The inscription on Hell. 5, which begins with a dedication to Athena Lindia and subsequently lists the names of officers and seamen of a number of *trihemioliai*, suggests that the consecration of the monument, like Hell. 4, resulted from a naval victory, possibly achieved with the assistance of the local manifestation of the goddess Athena.[56] According to Kinch, who reconstructed Hell. 5 in 1908,[57] traces of points of attachment for a statue were visible on the upper surface of the monument; however, in 1938 C. Blinkenberg stated that no such traces were preserved.[58] Blinkenberg assumed on the basis of the later popularity of the motif of a Victory figure alighting on a ship's prow that the crowning figure on Hell. 5 was also a Nike.[59]

However, in light of the monument's early date (for its type), the lack of evidence for precedent on Hell. 4, and the dedicatory inscription and its placement, the figure seems as likely to have been of Athena as of Victory.

Like its antecedents Hell. 4 and 5, Hell. 6 originally stood outside its sanctuary; in this case, behind and to the south of the theater at the Sanctuary of the Gods at Samothrace. It shares with Hell. 5 from Lindos the characteristic of having been manufactured of more than one type of stone: the base is said to be of *lithos larticos* from Rhodes, while the crowning Victory figure is considered to be made of Cycladic, possibly Parian, marble.[60] Hell. 6 is generally supposed to have been sculpted by the Rhodian Pythokritos and erected at Samothrace by Rhodians as a monument commemorating a naval victory ca. 200–180 B.C.; however, in the absence of literary or epigraphical evidence, it is not known which battle was commemorated.[61] The juxtaposition of local stone for the base and imported stone for the crowning statue was common among Rhodian sculptors of the Hellenistic period.[62] Hell. 6 is distinguished from its antecedents not only by its scale, quality of execution, and degree of preservation, but also by its oblique deployment as an element of an elaborate fountain group, in which real water replaced the marble waves of Hell. 4 and 5.[63] The far greater size and more elaborate setting for Hell. 6, complete with running water and rocks representing a promontory,[64] may be viewed as a unique example of the baroque style of Hellenistic art imposed upon the initially less ornate iconography of Hell. 4 and 5.[65]

Hell. 8, from in front of the Northeast Portico V in the east corner of the Agora of Thasos, is less ambitious than Hell. 6, but represents the same subject and is placed in an equally monumental setting. This base in the form of a prow, dated by its excavators to the second century B.C.,[66] floats over stylized waves, like Hell. 4 and 5, and when it was built, formed part of a votive monument surrounded by walls and benches on three sides. In the absence of epigraphical or literary evidence and its upper portions, which are not preserved, Hell. 8 may be presumed like Hell. 4–6 to have been a victory monument commemorating a naval battle. Although the battle is not known, it must have been of considerable consequence, judging from the overall size and the richness of the material. Hell. 8 and its marble enclosure were so large and centrally located that they virtually blocked direct access to the Northeast Portico V.[67]

Hell. 31, from the Agora of Cyrene, appears to represent the same genre of monument as Hell. 4–6 and 8. The dates of its erection and commemorative event are unknown, but are probably around the middle of the third century B.C.[68] Neither the precise location of Hell. 31 within the Agora of Cyrene nor the character of the original crowning statue is known; the fragments were found scattered throughout the agora and reconstructed upon an ancient base "of appropriate size,"[69] and the original statue is not preserved, although a Victory has been placed upon its platform.[70] The present reconstruction of Hell. 31 is manifestly incorrect; from the number and nature of the fragments it appears that two monuments may have been conflated into one.

Hell. 7, from the sculpture grotto at Sperlonga, is also of uncertain date and provenience. Most of the fragments were found concentrated in the vicinity of the large, centrally located pool within the grotto, but certain other fragments were discovered scattered throughout the grotto.[71] Scholars have proposed various dates for Hell. 7, ranging from the late third century B.C.[72] to the late first century A.C.[73] They have also proposed an equally broad range of possible reconstructions, including one in which the ship stands vertically on end, in the process of sinking.[74] Similarly, Hell. 7 and its associated sculptural groups have been ascribed to a number of sources, including a lost Hellenistic painting,[75] a work by the Rhodian sculptors of the Laocoon,[76] a literary source,[77] and a smaller sculpture in bronze or marble, suitably altered to fit the grotto setting.[78] It is also possible that Hell. 7 and its associated sculptures are wholly original, at least in execution.[79] Whatever its actual date of execution might be, the style and inspiration for Hell. 7 surely lie within the baroque period of Hellenistic art.[80]

The proveniences of other Hellenistic models tell less about their original functions. Thus, for example, Hell. 3, from a kiln dump in Gela, might have been intended for use by its manufacturer as a votive offering, a toy, a maritime souvenir, a burial offering, or a common household object, such as a lamp. Similarly, Hell. 37, found in a sondage in the harbor at Knidos, may have served as a votive offering, a jeweled pendant, a souvenir, or even an unusually elaborate net weight lost at the water's edge.[81] The proveniences for Hell. 33 and 34 are "Magnesia on the Maeander" and "Syria," respectively; despite the lack of more specific information, on the basis of their forms and diminutive size they may be assumed to have served as subsidiary decorative elements on pieces of sculpture or furniture. Hell. 35, 38, and 39 are of unknown provenience altogether and are therefore only tentatively included in the Hellenistic catalog. Their functions are unknown, although Hell. 38, in the form of a small bronze *aplustre*, is reminiscent of the miniature metal anchors from Delos and Rhenia, some of which served as burial offerings.[82]

CATALOG

Hell. 1. Rhyton in form of warship prow, from Vulci.

Ca. 400 B.C. (Göttlicher)

Hellenistic (Basch)

Late 4th–early 3d centuries B.C.

Function unknown (rhyton)

L: 20.3 cm; preserved H: 20.5 cm

London, British Museum D 201 (Blayds Collection, 1849)

Basch, 1969b:432, n. 4; 1975:207, fig. 13; Göttlicher, 1978:67, no. 360, pl. 27; *Walters, 1903:336–37, D 201. Walter cites "Mansell, *British Museum Photographs*, 772–773" (photographs of "the vase before restoration," according to Walters).

Hell. 1. Courtesy of the Trustees of the British Museum, London.

Rhyton in form of warship prow, of clay originally covered completely with black glaze. Entire vase heavily restored, including portions of stempost, handles, and mouth. Right arm, feet, and object in left hand of seated woman missing. Above flat bottom is wale, thickening toward bow. Wale ends in three-pronged ram in form of three superimposed dagger blades. Vertical strut supports and separates blades; base of strut is in form of lion's-head spout. Above ram wale is single strake; excrescences on starboard side possibly depict a flying dolphin. Above are three additional thickened wales, of which lowermost is composed of three horizontal timbers and two uppermost are fashioned of two horizontal timbers each. Two lower wales are separated by vertical members probably representing stanchions, as they do on Hell. 31. Leading ends of all three wales extend beyond stempost. On outside of bow compartment, a dolphin with oversized oculus and long bill; tail is obscured by restoration. Forward end of outrigger, which rests on middle wale as it does on Clas. 4, is decorated with female heads to either side. Draped woman seated against rhyton neck, which is otherwise decorated with reliefs of a reclining satyr playing the double flute, a maenad with thyrsos (?), and a winged Eros standing on a stepped plinth with his right elbow on the head of a draped female figure. Winged Eros figures also appear on Hell. 33 and 34, standing upon warship prows.

Hell. 2. Lamp in form of warship, from Greece.
Late 4th century B.C. (?)
Findspot unknown (lamp)
L: 13 cm; B: 4 cm; H: 9.1 cm
Seattle, Seattle Art Museum 62.158 (Cs6.14, acquired in 1962)

Unpublished. Mentioned by Anonymous, 1965, unpaginated, with photo; Hanfmann, in the work of Mitten and Doeringer, 1967:143, no. 148, with photograph.

Lamp in form of undecked warship, of combination solid and hollow cast bronze. Tips of stem- and sternposts, tip of lower *acrostolion* branch, and small portion of starboard rail and hull are missing. Articulated keel is flat forward of amidships, rising in steep curve to sternpost, which has high, two-branched *acrostolion*. Tip of ram is blunted and decorated with incised schematic boar's head with upright tusk on starboard side, "incised feathered line" to port. Above ram is lamp nozzle integrated into bow compartment, similar in placement to nozzles on Clas. 2 and 3. Top of nozzle is decorated

Hell. 2. Courtesy of the Seattle Art Museum, the Norman and Amelia Davis Classic Collection.

with triple torus molding. Single thick wale girdles hull, ending at aft edge of bow compartment. Gunwale marked by rounded molding in low relief. Lamp is only tentatively dated to the Hellenistic period; it could be from as early as the Archaic period, judging from the style of the incised boar's head.

Hell. 3. Boat model from midden or kiln dump, Gela, Sicily.
400 B.C. (Göttlicher)
310–280 B.C. (De Miro)
300–280 B.C. (*Adamesteanu)
Function unknown
L: 16 cm; B: 5.5 cm; L:B ratio: 2.9:1
Gela, Museo Archeologico Nazionale 3733

*Adamesteanu, 1954:130–31, pl. XXXIV.1–2; E. De Miro, personal communication, 1 August 1980; Göttlicher, 1978:67, no. 357, pl. 26; Orlandini, 1957:167, pl. LXXII.1.

Hell. 3. Courtesy of the Soprintendenza Archeologica, Agrigento, Sicily.

Model of undecked merchant (?) vessel, manufactured locally of reddish clay. Small portion of starboard bow missing; otherwise intact (reconstructed). Deep articulated keel is strongly rockered, at stern rising into single-branched *acrostolion*. Wide, beamy proportions. Stempost is thick at base, tapering to sharp point. Below and forward of stempost, a short thick projection represents either a ram or, as seems likelier in view of its height above the waterline and short length, a meeting of wales from either side. Horizontal ridges along hull in low relief may represent either strakes, modeling marks, or waves.

Hell. 4. Statue base in form of warship prow, from southeast corner of Building K, Agora of Epidauros.

4th century B.C. (Cavvadias)
Ca. 300 B.C. (*Blinkenberg)
Late 4th–early 3d centuries B.C. (Lehmann and Lehmann)
206 B.C.? (Göttlicher)
Statue base
Preserved L: 1.45 m; W: 32 cm (front); 64 cm (back); H: 95 cm (Göttlicher)
Preserved L: 1.52 m; width (W): 60 cm (front); 1.11 m (back); H: 81 cm (Werner)
Preserved L: 1.15 m; W: 32 cm (front); 70 cm (back); H: 52 cm (*Cavvadias)
Epidauros, in situ

*Blinkenberg, 1893:124, no. 13; 1938:32, n. 1, figs. 9–10; Bruneau,

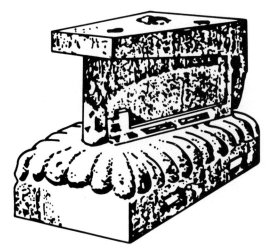

Hell. 4. Drawing by Vincent Amato, after Göttlicher, 1978.

1974:375, n. 106; Göttlicher, 1978:68–69, no. 368, pl. 28; *Cavva-dias, 1891:38–39, nos. 18–20; *Inscriptiones Graecae (IG)* IV² 306, A–D; Lehmann and Lehmann, 1973:193, n. 16, fig. 8; Marcadé, 1946:149, n. 2–3; Werner, 1975:99–100, with figures.

Statue base in form of schematized warship prow, of marble. Edge of stempost and tip of ram missing. Base comprises rectilinear block of marble with two lifting bosses on each side and one on back. Upper surface of base decorated with stylized wave pattern. Base is of coarser material and workmanship than prow. Prow rests on surface of waves; just above waterline is three-pronged ram in relief, abutting a rectangular feature. Behind, two wales separated by three diagonal struts or stanchions run from trailing edge of rectangular feature to back of base. Above ram and wales is smooth undecorated area, surmounted by a tapered slab, flat on its upper surface. The upper surface has four holes for attachment of statue (Victory?), two rounded holes on port side, and one foot-shaped hole on starboard side. Back is flat excepting lifting boss. Four inscriptions extant on sides of Hell. 4, of which three are well preserved (*IG* IV² 306, A–D).

Hell. 5. Statue base in form of warship prow, from back of east wall of stoa, Acropolis, Lindos, Rhodes.

265–260 B.C.

Statue base

Hell. 5. Courtesy of Prof. Donald White, University Museum, University of Pennsylvania, Philadelphia.

Preserved L: 1.80 m; preserved B: 1.60 m; preserved H: 1.60 m (Göttlicher)

Preserved L: 1.18 m; preserved B: 1.37 m; preserved H: 1.62 m (Werner)

Preserved L: 1.80 m; preserved B: 1.40 m; preserved H: 1.64 m (*Blinkenberg)

Lindos, in situ

*Blinkenberg 1938:30–37, 43–44, figs. 7–8, 11–12; 1941:301–3, no. 88, 1011, figs. 1–11; Bruneau, 1974:375, n. 106; *Göttlicher, 1978:68, no. 367, pl. 28; Lehmann and Lehmann, 1973:193–94, n. 17, fig. 9; Marcadé, 1946:147–52; Morrison, 1980:124–25, fig. 2; Werner, 1970:12, figs. 4–6.

Statue base in form of warship prow, of different marbles in four courses. Two lower courses of bluish-blackish marble; two upper courses of clear gray local *lithos larticos*. Tip of ram, most of second course, most of starboard outrigger, most of highest course missing; reconstructed remains are heavily restored. First (lowest) course comprises flattened base, into upper surface of which is carved an irregular wave pattern and lower section of hull. Second course includes a thick wale and, above, another section of hull. Third course represents outrigger, with flattened molding running unbroken from *epotis* around to lateral surface. Fourth (highest) course represents bow compartment. Some traces of fastening for crowning statue (Victory?) may or may not be preserved (see discussion in text). Lengthy inscription preserved on port side bow compartment records dedication to Athena Lindia and lists officers and crew of *trihemiolia* warships, from which it may be inferred that Hell. 5 represents a *trihemiolia*.

Hell. 6. Statue base in form of warship prow, from fountain near Sanctuary of the Gods, Samothrace.

Early 2d century B.C.

Statue base

Preserved L: 4.30 m; preserved B: 2.35 m; preserved H: 2.45 m

Paris, Louvre MA 2369

Anderson, 1962:25–31, frontispiece; Basch, 1969b:433–38, no. 2, fig. 5b (section); 1975:207; Bieber, 1955:125–26, figs. 92–96; Blin-

Hell. 6. Courtesy of the Louvre, Paris.

kenberg, 1938:37–40, fig. 13; Casson, 1971:102–3, 118–19, 129, n. 117, pl. 118 (detail of oarport); *Champoiseau, 1880:11ff, with photographs of unrestored bow; Couchoud and Svoronos, 1921:278, 286; Köster, 1923:146–49, figs. 31–33; Lehmann, 1955:71–73, fig. 6; *Lehmann and Lehmann, 1973:181–260; Marcadé, 1946:148–52; Moll, 1929:B II 83–83a; Morrison, 1980:125, fig. 4; Morrison and Williams, 1968:180, Hell. 3, 282–86, pl. 28; Rodgers, 1937:50–51, with three figures; Säflund, 1972:70; Sleeswyk, 1982:233–43 passim; Thiersch, 1931:337–56; Tilley, 1970:60–61, fig. 5; Torr, 1964; Werner, 1970:12–18, pl. II.2.

Statue base in form of warship prow, of gray *lithos larticos* from Rhodes.[83] Ram, portions of stempost, and bow compartment missing; marble surface chipped and abraded. Bow reconstructed and much restored (questionably). Rounded lower hull undecorated excepting a wide wale. *Epotis* of outrigger projects beyond lateral surface, unlike that on Hell. 5. Lateral outrigger surface has molding at top and bottom. Between moldings are pair of oarports in echelon, of horizontal oblong form, vertically bisected by thick tholepin. After end of oar box is attached to bow compartment by quarter-round strut, probably sculptural rather than architectural in derivation. Bow compartment has double horizontal molding, one at center and other along upper edge. Uppermost surface of bow compartment is flat.

Hell. 7. Sculpture group element in form of stern of ship, from sculpture grotto, Sperlonga, Italy.
Hellenistic (Jacopi, Säflund, 1966)
Late 3d–2d centuries B.C. (Lauter)
175–150 B.C. (G. M. A. Richter)
100 B.C. (*Conticello and Andreae)
Tiberian (von Blanckenhagen)
Late Claudian–early Flavian (*Säflund, 1972)
Neronian (Jacopi)
Sculpture group element
Dimensions unknown
Sperlonga, Sperlonga Museum

*Conticello and Andreae, 1974; Felbermeyer, 1971:136–45, with figures; Jacopi, 1966; Lauter, 1969:162–73; L'Orange, 1969:25–26; G. M. A. Richter, 1976:856; Säflund, 1966; *1972:8, 20, 44–56, 70, 97–98; Sichtermann, 1966:220–39; von Blanckenhagen, 1976:99–104.

Stern of ship of Rhodian *lithos larticos* (G. M. A. Richter). Portions of hull beneath steering oar and upper portion of *acrostolion* are missing; starboard side rough and unfinished. Reconstructed and heavily restored from many fragments. Stern comprises three alternating strakes and protruding wales, rising in steep curve to *acrostolion*. Stern railing supported by vertical stanchions in form of inverted L; spaces between two forward stanchions are solid, spaces aft are open. Steering oar box comprises flat upper surface, through which rounded upper end of angled steering oar protrudes at center. Lower edge of steering oar emerges from lower aft corner of box, below which a portion of the blade is preserved. Inscription on port side mentions Rhodian sculptors Athanodoros, Hagesandros, and Polydoros of the Hellenistic period, but inscription letter forms are dated to the Roman period.[84]

Hell. 8. Statue base in form of ship's prow, from east corner of agora, before Northeast Portico V, Thasos.
2d century B.C. (Anonymous, Bruneau)
Roman (Lehmann and Lehmann)
Votive statue base

Hell. 8. Courtesy of the École francaise d'Athènes, Athens, Greece.

Dimensions unknown

Thasos, Agora, in situ

Not fully published. Mentioned by Anonymous, 1950:348, fig. 65; 1967:27, fig. 6; Bruneau, 1974:375, fig. 22; Lehmann and Lehmann, 1973:196, n. 25.

Statue base in form of ship's prow, of two blocks of Thasian marble (Lehmann and Lehmann). Tip of bow and entire upper course missing. Forward edge of upper block dressed to abut ram is inscribed with the letters Δ and H. Probably warship, by analogy with Hell. 4–7 and 31. Prow rests on low rectilinear base decorated on either side with stylized curling waves suggesting motion (unlike Hell. 4 and 5). Upper surface roughly finished, with anathyrosis margin around edge for upper course. Three irregular holes on upper flat surface for attachment of missing course or possibly statue.

Hell. 9. Portion of funerary monument in form of warship prow, from eastern side of necropolis, Rhenia.

2d century B.C. (Göttlicher)

Late 2d–early 1st centuries B.C.

Funerary monument decoration

Preserved L: 98 cm; preserved B: 35 cm; preserved H: 42 cm

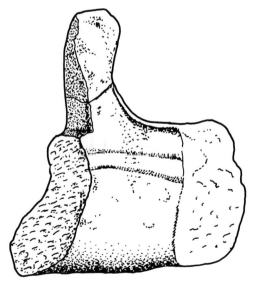

Hell. 9. Drawing by Frederick and Caroline Hemans, after Couilloud-Le Dinahet, 1978.

Rhenia, Necropolis, in situ

Couilloud–Le Dinahet, 1978:873, figs. 12D and 30; Couilloud, 1974: 344; Göttlicher, 1978:69, no. 368a, pl. 28; *Reinach, 1912:311–12, figs. 15–17; Werner, 1975:101.

Section of funerary monument in form of warship prow, of marble (possibly Parian).[85] Surface badly abraded; back unfinished. State of preservation is uncertain: Couilloud–Le Dinahet's 1978 photograph includes most of stempost but lacks ram and majority of bow; Göttlicher's 1978 drawing (after Werner) shows ram and stem intact, but lacks stempost. Presumably mortised into larger monument, judging from unfinished back surface. Dated by association with other Rhenian nautical funerary monuments, all of which are dated to the late second to early first centuries B.C.

Hell. 10. Warship prow from harbor (?), Ephesus.
Hellenistic
Function unknown
Preserved L: 81 cm; preserved B: 28 cm; preserved H: 68 cm
Selçuk, Archaeological Museum

*Lehmann and Lehmann, 1973:194, n. 20, figs. 12A–C.

Warship prow, of white island marble (Lehmann and Lehmann). Tip of ram, top of bow compartment, and rear of starboard side missing; surface abraded. Ram originally in form of three superimposed daggers, which form terminal of thick wale which tapers

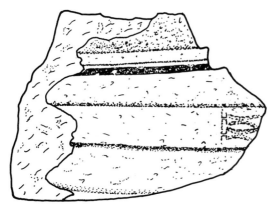

Hell. 10. Drawing by Frederick and Caroline Hemans, after Lehmann and Lehmann, 1973.

toward bow. Joint between hull and bow compartment marked by thick torus molding. In section, hull exhibits strong tumble home. Small dowel holes above ram and on top of bow compartment; square dowel hole on back for attachment to larger object.

Hell. 11. Sundial in form of warship prow, from southeast corner of gymnasium, Delos (found in 1911).
Hellenistic
Sundial decoration
L: 45 cm; B: 31.7 cm; H: 44.8 (18?) cm
Delos, Delos Museum B 4367

*Deonna, 1938:192–93, fig. 229, pl. LXVIII, nos. 548–49; Plassert, 1912:393–94, no. 8, pl. 5; Gibbs, 1976:89, 91, 189, no. 1072G, pls. 17–18.

Sundial of white marble, with south end in form of schematized warship prow. Ship portion is roughly finished; elsewhere, surface is polished. Below is a short ram, to the tip of which a broad wale extends. Above is another wale, ending also in short ram or *proembolon.* Above, additional pair of wales terminates in stempost, which is convex in profile. Wale continues unbroken around sundial to form upper and lower boundaries of outriggers. *Epotis* forms end of double hemispherical sundial, which is inscribed with day curves permitting

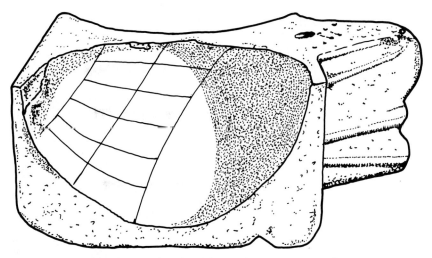

Hell. 11. Drawing by Frederick and Caroline Hemans, after Deonna, 1938.

it to be used both as a clock and as a calendar.[86] At tip of stempost is small hole for attachment of a stylus or possibly a small statue.[87] Another larger hole on upper flat surface ostensibly held a stylus. A gymnasium inventory of the second century B.C. may mention this sundial;[88] if so, the inventory would provide a terminus ante quem of the 2d century B.C. for Hell. 11.

Hell. 12. Funeral altar with warship prow, from Rhodes.
Hellenistic
Funerary function
L (of prow): ca. 46 cm; H (of altar): ca. 76.2 cm
Rhodes, Archaeological Museum

Göttlicher, 1978:67, no. 368b; *Lehmann and Lehmann, 1973:194, n. 21, figs. 13A–B; Werner, 1975:98–100, with four views.

Funerary altar with warship prow on upper surface, of gray marble. Tip of ram, stempost, and top missing. Surface of marble is rough and unpolished. Hull marked only by thickened wale running to tip of (missing) ram. Ram has hole at preserved end, possibly for attachment of bronze ram. Above, two wales at oblique angle

Hell. 12. Photograph by the author.

to keel run toward (missing) stempost. After ends of two upper wales merge into outrigger, the lower surface of which is perpendicular to the hull. Upper edge of bow compartment marked by double torus molding. Two round holes on upper surface of bow compartment for attachment of crowning statuette, now missing. Below, altar is decorated with double torus moldings at top and bottom, between which are bucrania connected with garlands in high relief. Altar may have been set into rock niche.[89]

Hell. 13. Warship prow from Asklepion (?), Kos.

Hellenistic

Function unknown

Preserved L: 40 cm; preserved B: 22 cm; preserved H: 34 cm

Kos, Archaeological Museum

*Lehmann and Lehmann, 1973:194, n. 18, fig. 10.

Warship prow of white marble. Entire bow and outermost surface of starboard outrigger missing.[90] Rough, unpolished surface. At bottom of hull to either side is a square hole for attachment of prow to base. Hull decorated only with thick horizontal wale. Above, two additional wales at oblique angle to keel run toward missing bow. Aftermost ends of upper wales merge into outrigger *epotis*, as they do on Hell 12. Above outrigger is bow compartment, upper edge of which is marked by a single torus molding. Back of prow is flat and roughly picked, with "swallow-tailed cutting for a Π-shaped clamp" (Lehmann and Lehmann).

Hell. 14. Lamp in form of warship, from Theater Quarter, Delos.

2d–1st centuries B.C.

Domestic context (?)

Preserved L: 38.6 cm; preserved B: 10.1 cm; preserved H: 3.9 cm

Delos, Delos Museum 4535

*Bruneau, 1965:107–8, no. 4535, pl. 27, no. 4535; Deonna, 1908: 172–73, figs. 39–40; Göttlicher, 1978:67, no. 361.

Lamp in form of decked warship, of brownish-gray micaceous clay with blackish matt glaze. Stempost and approximately half of central section of hull missing and restored in plaster. Slightly rockered keel rises gradually to blunt ram tip and sharply to sternpost, which is surmounted by inward-curving *acrostolion* with five branches

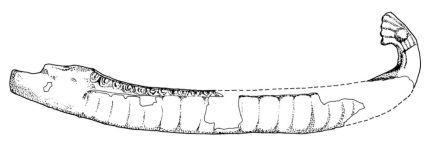

Hell. 14. Drawing by Frederick and Caroline Hemans, after Deonna, 1908.

and shield or boss on either side. Upper surface of ram has hole for lamp nozzle (filler hole?). Fifteen nozzles aligned along outrigger are restored to either side, separated by lateral incised lines. Upper surface of deck is subdivided by series of thwarts (benches?) bounded by a raised flat molding. Spaces between thwarts are either solidly filled or decorated with lozenge-shaped motifs, at least one of which is open, possibly to serve as filler hole. Around external edge of flat deck molding is a tongue motif.

Hell. 15. Lamp in form of warship, from east bank of Sacred Lake, Delos.
2d–1st centuries B.C.
Function unknown (lamp)
Preserved L: 9.8 cm
Delos, Delos Museum 4536
*Bruneau, 1965:108, no. 4536, pl. 27, no. 4536.

Fragmentary lamp in form of warship, of reddish-brown clay with similarly colored glaze. Ram, stempost, and short hull section preserved; remainder missing. Surface abraded. Blunted ram, with lamp nozzle on upper surface. High raked and inward-curved stempost, decorated along sides by incised lines around perimeter. Behind ram are *epotides* of outriggers to either side. Hull preserved to first thwart. Like that on Hell. 14, hull is decorated with tongue pattern outboard of thwarts.

Hell. 16. Lamp in form of warship, from Delos.
2d–1st centuries B.C.

Function unknown (lamp)

Preserved H: 11 cm

Delos, Delos Museum 4537

*Bruneau, 1965:108, no. 4537, pl. 27, no. 4537.

Fragmentary lamp in form of warship, of grayish clay with traces of black glaze. Sternpost and *acrostolion* preserved; remainder missing. Curved sternpost merges into five-branched *acrostolion*, of which the branch tips are separated. Small shield (boss?) with engraved circle in center covers middle three branches, as it does on Hell. 14.

Hell. 17. Lamp in form of warship, from Delos.

2d–1st centuries B.C.

Function unknown (lamp)

Preserved H: 7.1 cm

Delos, Delos Museum 4538

*Bruneau, 1965:108, no. 4538, pl. 27, no. 4538.

Fragmentary lamp in form of warship, of gray clay with black glaze. Top of five-branched *arostolion* with separated tips preserved; remainder missing. Small shield (boss?) with engraved circle in center covers middle three branches, as it does on Hell. 14 and 16.

Hell. 18. Lamp in form of warship, from Delos.

2d–1st centuries B.C.

Function unknown (lamp)

Dimensions unknown

Delos, Delos Museum 4539

Unpublished. Mentioned by Bruneau, 1965:107–8.

Fragmentary lamp in form of warship; state of preservation unknown. Analogous in form to other ship-shaped lamps from Delos (Bruneau).

Hell. 19. Lamp in form of warship, from Delos.

2d–1st centuries B.C.

Function unknown (lamp)

Preserved L: 6.3 cm

Delos, Delos Museum 4540

*Bruneau, 1965:108, no. 4540, pl. 27, no. 4540.

Lamp in form of warship, of red clay. Small portion of deck preserved; remainder missing. Preserved are two thwarts and one end of hull interior, surrounded by cord pattern.

Hell. 20. Lamp in form of warship, from west of Agora of Italians, Delos.

2d–1st centuries B.C.

Function unknown (lamp)

Preserved L: 12.2 cm; preserved B: 9.3 cm; preserved H: 3.2 cm

Delos, Delos Museum 4541

*Bruneau, 1965:108, no. 4541, pl. 27, no. 4541.

Fragmentary lamp in form of warship, of light brown clay with black glaze. Fragment comprises lower portion of stern and hull at stern; remainder missing. Surface abraded. Two horizontal projections, one at either side of stern, each with two incised lines on upper surface, represent steering oars within oar box. Preserved section of outrigger incorporates single lamp nozzle, as on Hell. 14.

Hell. 21. Lamp in form of warship, from House of Comedians, Delos.

2d–1st centuries B.C.

Domestic context

Dimensions unpublished

Delos, Delos Museum 4541 bis

Unpublished. Mentioned by Bruneau, 1965:108.

Fragmentary lamp in form of warship. Analogous to Hell. 20 (Delos, Delos Museum 4541).

Hell. 22. Lamp in form of ship, from Delos.

2d–1st centuries B.C.

Function unknown (lamp)

Preserved L: 8.1 cm; preserved B: 5.2 cm

Delos, Delos Museum 4542

*Bruneau, 1965:108, no. 4542, pl. 27, no. 4542.

Fragmentary lamp in form of ship, of light brown clay with black glaze. Small section of deck preserved; remainder missing. Decoration consists of floral pattern of two pairs of laurel leaves alternating with single palmette in low relief. On one side, pair of small holes; on other side, two larger holes on raised clay band. Probably fragment of same model as Hell. 23.

Hell. 23. Lamp in form of ship, from Delos.
2d–1st centuries B.C.
Function unknown (lamp)
Preserved L: 8.5 cm
Delos, Delos Museum 4543

*Bruneau, 1965:108, no. 4543, pl. 27, no. 4543.

Fragmentary lamp in form of ship, of brown clay. Small section of deck preserved, comprising two thwarts bordered by raised fillet, rectangular in section, narrowing toward one end. Beside thwart is floral motif of alternating pairs of laurel leaves and single palmette, as on Hell. 22. Probably fragment of same model as Hell. 22.

Hell. 24. Lamp in form of ship, from Delos.
2d–1st centuries B.C.
Function unknown (lamp)
Preserved L: 9.5 cm
Delos, Delos Museum 4544

*Bruneau, 1965:108–9, no. 4544, pl. 27, no. 4544.

Fragmentary lamp in form of ship, of gray clay with black glaze. Portion of deck preserved; remainder missing. Deck comprises pair of wide raised thwarts, separated by solid raised lozenge motif with dot in center. To either side of lozenge are open oblong (filler?) holes. Thwarts bounded by raised molding, rectangular in section, outside of which is raised cord pattern. Outside cord pattern are stubs of one partial and four complete lamp nozzles. Probably fragment of same model as Hell. 25.

Hell. 25. Lamp in form of ship, from Delos.
2d–1st centuries B.C.
Function unknown (lamp)
Preserved L: 7.6 cm
Delos, Delos Museum 4544 bis

*Bruneau, 1965:108–9, no. 4544 bis, pl. 27, no. 4544 bis.

Fragmentary lamp in form of ship, of gray clay with black glaze. Like Hell. 24, except that portions of cord pattern are preserved on either side of vessel's thwart. Probably fragment of same model as Hell. 24.

Hell. 26. Lamp in form of warship, from Delos.
2d–1st centuries B.C.
Function unknown (lamp)
Preserved L: 13.9 cm; preserved B: 7.4 cm; preserved H: 3.4 cm
Delos, Delos Museum 4545

*Bruneau, 1965:109, no. 4545, pl. 27, no. 4545.

Fragmentary lamp in form of warship, of gray clay with black and brown glaze. Section of bow preserved; remainder missing. Ram surmounted by inward-curving stempost, which in plan merges without break into outriggers. Along upper outrigger surface are one fragmentary and two complete nozzles, separated by incised lines representing oars. Between outriggers is open space with round (filler?) hole, circumscribed by raised fillet in low relief. Fillet is rectangular at forward end, unlike analogous features on Hell. 14, 15, 19, 23, 27, 29, and 30.

Hell. 27. Lamp in form of ship, from Rue de l'Est, Delos.
2d–1st centuries B.C.
Function unknown (lamp)
Preserved L: 16.6 cm; B: 5.3 cm; preserved H: 3 cm
Delos, Delos Museum 4546

*Bruneau, 1965:109, no. 4546, pl. 27, no. 4546.

Fragmentary lamp in form of ship, of gray clay with black glaze. Bow (?) and forward (?) section of deck missing. Preserved end (stern?) rises in low curve to pointed terminal. Deck, which is offset by rounded raised fillet, is pierced by three (filler?) holes in center; central hole surrounded by raised round fillet. Port (?) side pierced by eight (preserved) lamp nozzles; starboard (?) side has seven (preserved) nozzles. Originally, there appear to have been nine nozzles per side.

Hell. 28. Lamp in form of ship, from Delos.
2d–1st centuries B.C.
Function unknown (lamp)
Preserved L: 8 cm
Delos, Delos Museum 4547
*Bruneau, 1965:109, no. 4547, pl. 27, no. 4547.

Fragmentary lamp in form of warship, of gray clay with black glaze. One end (bow?) preserved; remainder missing. In plan, one side (starboard?) bulges slightly, possibly portraying an outrigger; if so, Hell. 28 is a warship. On upper surface, three lamp nozzles preserved.

Hell. 29. Lamp in form of warship, from south of Agora of Italians, Delos.
2d–1st centuries B.C.
Function unknown (lamp)
Preserved L: 12.9 cm; B: 6.1 cm; preserved H: 3 cm
Delos, Delos Museum 4548
*Bruneau, 1965:109, no. 4548, pl. 27, no. 4548.

Lamp in form of decked warship, of red-brown clay with black glaze. Sternpost missing; otherwise intact. Proportionately oversized ram has round lamp nozzle on upper surface. Ram merges into outriggers, each of which has three lamp nozzles. To either side of nozzles are incised lines, possibly representing oars. Deck spanned by four thwarts; spaces between three are solidly filled, other two are pierced by elliptical (filler?) holes. A pair of raised moldings, possibly representing gunwales, circumvent thwarts.

Hell. 30. Lamp in form of warship, from Delos.
2d–1st centuries B.C.
Function unknown (lamp)

Preserved L: 11.5 cm

Delos, Delos Museum 4549

Unpublished. Mentioned by Bruneau, 1965:109, no. 4549.

    Lamp in form of decked warship, of light brown clay with brown or blackish glaze. Sternpost and ram missing; starboard side badly preserved. "Exact analogue, in form and dimensions," to Hell. 29 (Bruneau).

Hell. 31. Naval monument with base in form of warship prow, from Agora, Cyrene.

246–241 B.C. (Ermeti)

Hellenistic (Marcadé)

1st century B.C.

Early 1st century B.C. (Fuchs)

Monument base

Dimensions unknown

Cyrene, Agora, in situ

Hell. 31. Courtesy of Dr. Murray McClellan, University Museum, University of Pennsylvania, Philadelphia.

Basch, 1969b:432, n. 4; 1975:208, fig. 16; Bruneau, 1974:375, n. 106; Caputo, 1968:230–33; *Ermeti, 1981; Fuchs, 1942:27–28, pl. 7; Goodchild, 1963:49, plan no. 26; Göttlicher, 1978:81, no. 485, pl. 37; Lehmann and Lehmann, 1973:196, n. 23, fig. 14; Marcadé, 1946:49–51; Stucchi, 1959; 1967:84–93, figs. 61–71; Werner, 1970:18, fig. 23; White, in the work of R. Stillwell, 1976:254.

Naval monument in form of warship prow, of white marble in several courses. In numerous fragments, heavily restored in brick and stone, manifestly incorrectly. As restored, at base on either side is a dolphin supporting the superstructure. Resting on dolphins, a ram formed of three superimposed blades, as on Hell. 1 and 32. Blades are joined at haft into trident, with two bosses at base of blades, as on Hell. 32. Above is hull of ship, covered by eagle. Three superimposed wales above hull are separated by widely spaced stanchions. Wales project well beyond stempost, as on a modern bowsprit. Rectangular plates or panels decorated with female busts adorn wales. Above are portions of gunwale and stempost incorrectly placed. Aft of bow section, a portion of the outrigger is preserved with partially preserved oblong oarport, as on Hell. 6. It appears that more than one monument has been incorporated into Hell. 31.

Hell. 32. Warship ram, from Rhodes.
Hellenistic
Function unknown
Preserved L: 53 cm; preserved B: 21 cm; preserved H: 28 cm
(Lehmann and Lehmann)

Hell. 32. Photograph by the author.

Preserved L: 55 cm; preserved B: 26 cm; preserved H: 30.5 cm
(Göttlicher)
Rhodes, Archaeological Museum

Basch, 1975:207, fig. 14; Göttlicher, 1978:69, no. 368c, pl. 29; Lehmann and Lehmann, 1973:194, n. 19, fig. 11.

Ram of warship, of gray Rhodian marble (Lehmann and Lehmann). Ram only is preserved; remainder missing. Articulated keel rises in straight line to tip of ram. Ram in form of three superimposed blades joined at haft into trident. Two bosses present at base of blades, as on Hell. 31. Back of ram is flat, originally for attachment to larger monument.

Hell. 33. Furniture attachment in form of warship prow, from Magnesia on the Maeander.
Hellenistic (Göttlicher)
Furniture decoration
H: 11.3 cm
Berlin, Antiquarium 8929 (lost?)

Göttlicher, 1978:68, no. 366; Marcadé, 1946:149, n. 7; *Pernice, 1904:29, no. 31, fig. 31.

Furniture (or vessel?) attachment in form of warship prow, of bronze. Schematic prow comprises flat pointed ram with strongly curved stempost above. Incised lines along prow probably represent joints between strakes. Plump winged Eros figure with extended wings and pointed cap stands on prow; left hand holds ball with attached laced handle, identified by Pernice as a *malagma*, or ship fender. Right hand possibly holds lace for fastening ball onto handle. Lines along hull more closely resemble Roman than Hellenistic ship representations.[91]

Hell. 34. Ship prow, from Syria.
Hellenistic (Göttlicher)
Function unknown
Dimensions unknown
Present location unknown

*De Ridder, 1905:55ff., pl. VI; Göttlicher, 1978:68, no. 365; Marcadé, 1946:149, n. 8.

Ship's prow, of bronze. Eros figure stands on top, as on Hell. 33. Either a furniture or vessel ornament, or possibly a *lar* (Marcadé). If the latter, then Hell. 34 would date to the Roman period, since the *lar* was a Roman household god.

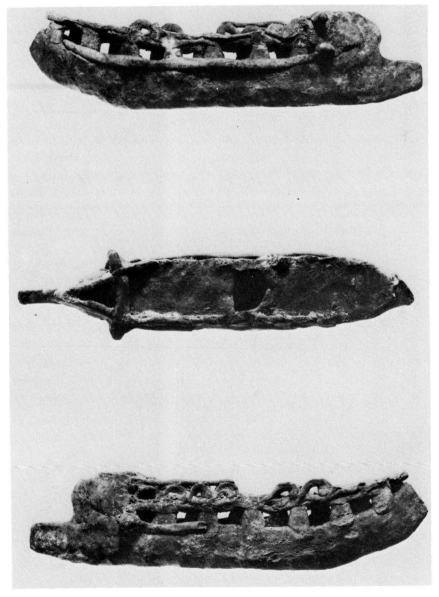

Hell. 35. Courtesy of the Master and Fellows of Corpus Christi College, Cambridge, England.

Hell. 35. Warship model.

Before 500 B.C. (Köster)

Classical, possibly Hellenistic (Morrison and Williams)

Hellenistic (Basch, Kirk)

3d–1st centuries B.C. (Göttlicher)

Function unknown

L: 20 cm

Cambridge, Corpus Christi College

Basch, 1968a:166–71, pl. 8; 1969a:238–39, fig. 27; de Graeve, 1978: 243, n. 1, fig. 179; *Froener, 1878:20, no. 154; Göttlicher, 1978: 68, no. 363, pl. 27; Kirk, 1949:116, n. 29; Köster, 1923:88–89, fig. 19; Morrison and Williams, 1968:49, 179, Clas. 21.

Model of warship, of light-colored clay. Stempost, portions of upper deck rail, and sternpost missing; keel chipped at turn of sternpost from keel. Keel is flat, rising in low curve to stempost; slight rise also to ram, which is blunted. Diagonal marks along hull in low relief may represent either hull bindings[92] or, as seems likelier, stylized waves[93] or artist's finger marks. Upper edge of hull marked by thickened line: either a wale or gunwale. Toward bow, at wale or gunwale level, is a thwart projecting beyond the sides of the hull: possibly the leading edge of the outrigger, a cathead, or a structural thwart. Above wale or gunwale is a series of thickened stanchions supporting a deck. Deck surface is curved upward at stem; at its midpoint is a D-shaped hatch or mast step. Along edges of deck to either side, a wavy applied strip of clay with a horizontal applied strip along its upper surface: probably a rail or possibly a series of schematized oarports. Bow compartment extends above deck level and has a thwart spanning its trailing edge. Eye or shield in low relief on port side bow screen. Model may represent a *penteres* (Basch).

Hell. 36. Model of *trieres*, from Erment, Egypt.

4th–3d centuries B.C. (Barnett)

Ca. 350 B.C. (Göttlicher)

350 B.C. or later (Bass)

Hellenistic (Morrison and Williams, *Breitenstein)

Function unknown

L: 39 cm; H: 12.6 cm

Copenhagen, National Museum 5487 (acquired in 1902 from Cairo dealer)

Alexanderson, 1914:38, pl. III; Barnett, 1958:229, pl. XXIVd; Basch,

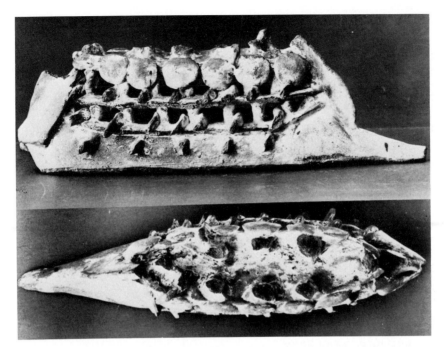

Hell. 36. Courtesy of the National Museum, Department of Near Eastern and Classical Art, Copenhagen.

1966:115, 122; 1969a:158–59, 232–34, fig. 16, pl. 9; 1975:210, fig. 21; Bass, 1972:47, 58, pl. 14; *Breitenstein, 1941:56, no. 520, pl. 63; Casson, 1971:94–95, figs. 103–4; de Graeve, 1978:242–43, n. 3, fig. 178; Frost, 1975: 226; Lloyd, 1975:46–48, pl. VIIa; Morrison and Williams, 1968:180, Hell. 1, pl. 27c.

Model of three-banked *trieres*, of dark reddish-brown clay with white slip. Traces of red and black glaze. Oars, terminals of stem- and sternposts, and attachments (figures?) on upper deck missing. Surface abraded. Flat bottom, with narrow elongated ram, blunted at tip, extending horizontally from keel. Thick stempost, convex in profile, is canted aft. In section, hull exhibits strong tumble home, with widest beam at lower oar bank. At point of maximum beam, below gunwale level, five oar stubs protrude from hull. Above, an incised line along hull separates wale from gunwale. Seven deck stanchions set into gunwale, possibly representing extensions of interior frames. On port side, seven oar stubs of middle oar bank are fastened to trailing edge of stanchions, which therefore double as tholepins. On starboard side, of seven oar stubs of middle bank, five are attached to stanchion's trailing edges, two to leading edges. Above stanchions, a horizontal longitudinal member represents a deck or railing over which the upper oar bank is plied. Second level of stanchions is not set directly over lower level; some are set midway between. On port side, four oar stubs on upper bank are all set against trailing edges of stanchions; on starboard side, seven of eight oar stubs abut the trailing edges and one is set against the leading edge. Upper level of stanchions abuts a horizontal member, which doubles as an upper deck and railing; six round shields are attached to this member on either side. Upper deck is flat, with three opposed pairs of stubs of vertical objects (figures of rowers or marines?) set into deck. Pair of thick oversized steering oars is canted diagonally aft, one oar to either side. According to Basch, the presence of the convex stempost, the shields, the absence of outriggers and wales, and the oversized ram identify Hell. 36 as a Phoenician *trieres*.[94]

Hell. 37. Warship model from harbor sondage, Knidos.
Hellenistic (?)
Function unknown
Dimensions unknown
Present location unknown

Unpublished. Mentioned by its excavator, Iris Love, at the annual Archaeological Institute of America/American Philological Association meetings, Atlanta, Georgia, in December 1977.

Warship model of bronze.

Hell. 38. Acrostolion or *aplustre.*
Hellenistic or later (Diels)
Function unknown
H: 10.5 cm
Present location unknown (formerly Berlin, Antiquarium 1328)

Anonymous, 1924–32:89; *Diels, 1915:62, n. 1, fig. 1; Göttlicher, 1978:85, no. 511; Moll, 1929:B IX 28.

Six-branched *acrostolion* or *aplustre*, of bronze. Tips of second highest and lowest branches missing; surface heavily corroded. Branches are joined at base, separating midway along length. Branches joined near tops by straight bar and pointed near tips.

Hell. 39. Warship model.
Hellenistic (?)
Function unknown

L: 13 cm

Paris, Louvre CA 1250

*Göttlicher, 1978:85, no. 512, pl. 40.

Warship model, of clay. Ram and stern missing; surface abraded at bow. Line of keel sharply rounded at stern; ram is depicted as straight extension of keel. In section, hull is slightly convex. Model is solid, giving appearance of decked vessel. Gunwale articulated by rounded molding, rising into vertical stempost. On deck near bow, two small protuberances, presumably representing remnants of features now missing. Toward stern and below gunwale level, short outrigger is preserved. Possibly of the Hellenistic period or later.

7

Conclusions

In the preceding chapters, more than 131 ship and boat models, and in Appendix II at least 6 representations of additional models, are cataloged for the years between the beginning of the Bronze Age and the end of the Hellenistic period. The figure of 137 examples, however, is virtually meaningless, since it is only an indeterminate fraction of the total number of models actually produced. To it may be added, for example, models unexcavated to date, models not recognized as such by their respective excavators, models too fragmentary to be properly identified, unpublished models, models made of perishable materials that have not been preserved, and models destroyed in antiquity.

The popularity of ship and boat models varies widely among the traditional historical periods of Greek antiquity. For example, more models have been found from the Bronze Age and Archaic and Hellenistic periods than from the intervening Geometric and Classical periods. The decline in numbers for the Geometric period may be explained as a manifestation of a generalized cultural decline after the end of the Bronze Age, a decline during which production of all sorts of minor arts decreased. No such explanation exists for the radical decline in the number of models for the Classical period, nor is one offered here; it may only be reiterated that in this period, evidence of seafaring was extremely limited in all forms but written ones. The numbers increase once again in the Hellenistic period and continue to grow in Roman times (see Appendix III).

So far, the models from each of the traditional historical periods have been viewed primarily in the context of their particular periods. However, when viewed as a corpus, the models exhibit several generalized trends. One of the most conspicuous of these trends concerns the models' proveniences: slightly more than three-quarters of the corpus with known findspots are from the Greek islands. For instance, for the Bronze Age, only 5 of 27 models were found on mainland Greece, while 12 of the 27, nearly half of the total number for the entire period, were found on Crete. Numerical proportions are similar for the Geometric period, from which three-quarters of the models with known proveniences were found on Crete and the remainder on the mainland. Likewise, for the Archaic period, 22 of a total of 53 models were found on the island of Samos alone.[1] Only during the Classical period does model production not conform to the insular orientation; however, too few models are known from this period as yet to establish any definitive source of production. Lastly, of a total of 36 cataloged models with known proveniences from the Hellenistic period, 26 are from island sites; of these, fully 20 come from Delos or Rhenia. It appears from these figures that the island settlements as a group placed a greater emphasis upon seafaring than did their mainland counterparts, an emphasis that filtered down into local artistic production.[2]

Another prominent trend is evident in the choice of materials. Throughout Greek antiquity, the most popular material for ship and boat models was terracotta. Of the 128 models whose materials have been identified, 70 are of terracotta.[3] Half or more of the models from each historical period are of terracotta, excepting only the Geometric period, for which the figure is one-quarter.[4] Terracotta is followed in descending order of popularity by wood (22 models), marble (12 models), bronze (11 models), and lead, iron, and unidentified stone (4 models each). A single model (BA 16) may be made of ivory; however, aside from this example no Greek models made of precious materials are known except through written sources (see Appendix I). The popularity of terracotta as a material for such a high proportion of models is understandable: it was omnipresent, easily refined and modeled, and durable. It is far more surprising that as many as 22 wooden models have survived from antiquity, for although wood is as easily procured and modeled as clay, it is far less durable. Marble, the third most popular material, was not used for watercraft models until the Hellenistic period, but at that time it was widely used; nearly one-third of the known Hellenistic models were made of marble. Marble is closely followed in popularity by bronze, with 11 examples. Together, bronze and terracotta were the only materials used for models in every historical period of Greek antiquity. The opposite is true for the less popular metals, lead and iron. Each of these was used for models in only a single period: lead in the Bronze Age and iron in the Geometric period.

Another distinct trend emerges over time in regard to the architecture of the models. Except for the Bronze Age examples, most Greek watercraft models fall into three broad architectural categories: small craft, merchant vessels, and warships. Thus far, the Bronze Age evidence, comprising both two- and three-dimensional representations, is ambiguous concerning the latter two types: no clear distinction is made between merchant vessels and warships. In the absence of evidence to the contrary, therefore, it may be inferred that during the Bronze Age the same ships were used for both military and commercial purposes, as has occurred in more recent times.[5] Beginning with the Geometric period, however, the evidence becomes clearer: distinctive warships began to be built, with long, narrow proportions and rams at the bow. From this period onward, warships predominate among models of discernible ship types by a margin of almost 10 to 1, with 95 definite and 9 probable examples. Small craft models are a distant second, with only 11 definite examples and 1 possible example. From the Geometric through the Hellenistic periods, only 2 merchant vessels are positively identified. This bias toward warships among post–Bronze Age models clearly reflects the tastes and preferences of both the craftsmen who formed the models and the individuals who acquired and used them. It may be inferred that those who used the models were connected in some way with naval service, possibly as marines, naval officers, or common seamen. It is also possible that warships were less common in daily life than merchant craft, and that their comparative rarity guaranteed their greater popularity among models. The prevalence of the warship over the merchant vessel may also indicate the model's specific intended function. For instance, a warship with its protruding ram and oar bays might more easily be adapted for use as a lamp than might a merchantman without these characteristics.

Certain trends are also evident in the functions of the models. As has been discussed in previous chapters, ship and boat models in ancient Greece had three primary functions: they served as votives, as objects connected with a variety of funerary practices, and as ship-shaped common household articles, such as lamps or drinking vessels. Of the 78 models with known proveniences, 43 were used as votives or as bases for votive statues; another 8 examples are designated as probable votives. This tentative total of 51 votives, equaling two-thirds of the models with known proveniences, represents the largest functional category within the corpus. In addition, it is the only category that appears in every historical period of Greek antiquity. The first use of watercraft models as votives appears in the Middle Minoan period on Crete; by the Late Bronze Age this function had spread to other Aegean islands and to the mainland as well. During the Geometric period, the geographical distribution of votive models was limited to Crete alone, but by the Archaic period, production had resumed on the mainland and among the Aegean islands and had begun in Anatolia and at overseas settlements. Just over three-fifths of all of the Archaic models (32 of 53) served as votives. After the Archaic period, however, production of votive models declined; there are only two examples from the Classical period and only two certain and five tentative examples from the Hellenistic period. By the latter period, votive models tended not to be small-scale three-dimensional objects, but rather bases for votive statues or subsidiary decorative elements of large-scale sculpture groups.

After votives, the next most prevalent function for models was that of funerary objects, with 18 examples. During the Bronze Age, these were burial offerings, but later, in the Hellenistic period, they also appeared as subsidiary elements of funerary monuments. Proportionately, the most popular era for ship models used as burial offerings was the Geometric period; six of a total of eight examples appeared in this context. This function was least popular in the Archaic and Classical periods, during both of which only a single example appeared, and that in western Anatolia (Arch. 1, from Sardis). Similarly, only two funerary models, both in the form of subsidiary ornamental components of funerary sculptures, are known from the Hellenistic period.

Models from domestic contexts represent the smallest functional category for models within the corpus, with a total of only nine examples. Six of these date to the Bronze Age; the other three are from Hellenistic Delos.[6] No models from domestic contexts are known from the Geometric through the Classical periods. For those nine domestic models from the Bronze Age and Hellenistic period, the specific functions are not positively identified and may overlap with the votive and funerary categories. Such an overlap might occur, for instance, if a model had been deposited after its manufacture and acquisition but before its intended application. In any case, the numbers of models in the various functional categories clearly demonstrate that domestic use was far less common than votive or funerary use by a wide margin.

The remaining 53 cataloged models are either from unknown contexts or are from such nonspecific proveniences that their functions remain virtually unknown. This unknown category is larger by two examples than the next largest group, comprising votives. Obviously, if the functions of the models from unknown contexts were known, they might totally alter the relative proportions of the three primary functional categories. They might also provide a few new categories, as did the models from the written sources (see Appendix I). For example, 14 of the models, all from the Potters' Quarter in Corinth, might legitimately be placed in the domestic functional category, since the Potters' Quarter comprises mainly individual dwellings with associated workshops or work areas.[7]

The significance of ancient Greek watercraft models may be approached from a number of perspectives. As a class of objects among the minor arts, they reflect one of the most widespread and longest-lasting cultural traits of the ancient Greeks: their close relationship with and dominance over the sea. Ships were the fastest, safest, and most economical means of transportation available to the ancient Greeks; without them they could not have traded, traveled, or communicated over long distances or made war or enforced the peace to the extent that they did. Among the various sorts of nautical imagery with which the Greeks surrounded themselves, watercraft models occupied a special niche; they were used as toys during childhood, as both sacred and profane objects during maturity, and as funerary objects at death. These models, particularly the larger monumental examples, also had a profound impact upon all subsequent nautical imagery in the Western world, an impact that has lasted into the twentieth century (see Appendix III).

Ships, which represent the combined efforts of a variety of highly specialized skills and trades, were among the most technologically complex mechanisms of the ancient world. Warships were at the forefront of this technology; of the various types of watercraft, they evolved most rapidly, in order for the states that designed and deployed them to maintain a strategic and tactical advantage over their enemies. Thus, from their origins in the Middle Geometric to early Archaic periods until the end of the Hellenistic period, when they passed into general disuse, warships developed from simple single-level floating projectiles into massive battleships with crews numbering in the hundreds and a variety of weapons in their arsenals.

The extent of modern knowledge of ancient ships is inversely proportional to their social, political, and economic importance; as was stated earlier, most of the representational, written, and archaeological sources of information provide very little substantive data. Three-dimensional models, on the other hand, the vast majority of which are in the form of warships, help bridge the gap in our understanding of these most complex and critical historical factors—the ships themselves.

Appendixes

I

Written Sources

The written sources for Greek ship and boat models may be put into two categories: epigraphical and literary. Although neither category is especially large, together these sources provide new information about models and confirm some of the hypotheses outlined in earlier chapters.

EPIGRAPHICAL EVIDENCE

The epigraphical evidence is limited primarily to inventory lists of offerings made at the Artemision and at the Temple of Apollo on Delos. The earliest list, dating to 364 B.C., contains a single reference to an unspecified number of *"trieres*-like kraters" dedicated at the Artemision.[1] It does not describe the materials, sizes, weights, donors, or dates of dedication of the kraters, and neither do the other Artemision votive inventories. Aside from the vessels referred to in this one inscription, no vessel as large as a krater and shaped like a *trieres* is known from ancient Greece.

Beginning as early as 300–280 B.C. and continuing at least until 180 B.C., a group of inventory lists for the Temple of Apollo catalog a silver *trieres* dedicated by the Hellenistic ruler Seleukos I, who ruled between 305 and 281 B.C.[2] The earliest list, dating to the archonship of Hypsokles, gives the weight of the *trieres* as 1520 drachmas, or 6.54 kilograms at the Attic standard of 4.30 grams per drachma.[3] However, a slightly later list, dating to 279 B.C., gives for the same *trieres* a weight of more than 1544 drachmas, or 6.64 kilograms (the end of the weight notation is missing).[4] The weight discrepancy between the two inventories may perhaps be ascribed to a difference in mensuration techniques or standards (Attic versus Delian?) or to measurements with and without associated attachments (rigging, oars, etc). If the *trieres* was an actual replica of a warship and not, for example, a rhyton with naval attributes, as appears to be the case in light of its weight, it would certainly have been one of the largest known ship models from antiquity.

One Delian inventory, dated to 153/52 B.C., refers to a *tetreres* dedicated by Seleukos which weighed 1700 drachmas, or 7.31 kilograms, with its "little bronze cables preserved."[5] The *tetreres* appears at the same spot in the sequence of votive offerings at the Temple of Apollo as does the silver *trieres* in the other inventories. Its position in the sequence led F. Durrbach to conclude that it and the *trieres* were the same model.[6] However, the weight difference, the absence of the material, and the presence of the bronze cables suggest that the *tetreres* model was a different object. The presence of the cables further indicates that the *tetreres* was a ship replica rather than a rhyton or drinking vessel. If the weight notation was not merely an error on the part of the engraver of the inscription, the *tetreres* would have been even larger than the silver *trieres*.

LITERARY EVIDENCE

Homer, writing in the late eighth century B.C., makes the earliest reference to ship models in Greek literature.[7] In *The Iliad* (11.20), he relates that Kinyras of Paphos (Cyprus) fulfilled his promise to supply Agamemnon with 50 ships in the Trojan War by sending 49 clay models aboard one real ship. (After the war ended, Agamemnon rewarded Kinyras for his cleverness by banishing him to Amathus.)

The Byzantine historian Prokopios mentions another ship model associated with Agamemnon. In his *History of the Wars* (VIII.22, 27–29), Prokopios says that a votive ship model made of many stones and dedicated at Geraistos in Euboea was erected by Agamemnon, both to atone for the Greek insult to Artemis and to commemorate the Greek fleet sailing against Troy. In the mid sixth century A.C., when Prokopios wrote about the model, the first two verses of the hexametric inscription were still legible, as was the last line, which recorded the name of the model's sculptor, Tynnichos. Prokopios asserts that the inscription was carved either at the time of the ship's dedication or later; on philological grounds the preserved verses have been attributed to the sixth century B.C.[8] If the inscription is as early as has been suggested, the Geraistos votive model would antedate the earliest preserved monumental ship sculpture (Hell. 4) by as much as two centuries.

Earlier in the same passage, Prokopios refers to a ship model made of white stone and erected by the shore in the land of the Phaiakians.[9] In Prokopios's time, some thought this Phaiakian model to be the petrified remains of the ship that bore Odysseus back to Ithaca. However, Prokopios himself properly rejects this story, noting that the ship was not monolithic but was composed of many stones and that an inscription named the merchant who had built the ship as a votive to Zeus Kasios. The model was presumably built and dedicated after a successful and possibly hazardous trading voyage.

Another such monument, dedicated at a sanctuary at Elaious in the Thracian Chersonesos, is of a naval rather than mercantile derivation. It is mentioned in passing by the third century A.C. author Philostratus in *Heroikos*. (III.2) as a "statue [of Protesilas] erected at [the] temple, set up by a nauarch, the foot of which is in the form of a prow [sic]."[10] Although Philostratus says nothing else, it may be assumed from the donor's title that a successful naval battle lay behind the dedication.

Pliny (*Natural History*, VII.21) makes a single reference to a ship model of the Archaic period. According to Pliny, a certain Myrmekides made a boat "quam apicula pinnis absconderet" ("which a bee in flight made off with"). Myrmekides, a sculptor and engraver of the Archaic period from either Athens or Miletus, was famous as an artist of miniature objects.[11] Although no precise parallels for Myrmekides's boat are known from ancient Greece, a pair of small golden warship pendants attributed to Phoenician workmanship is displayed in the Louvre.[12]

Aristophanes and Plutarch make two references to fifth century B.C. ship models. The earlier reference, in Aristophanes's *Clouds* (879), provides evidence that models served as children's toys, a function that has been suggested but never actually proven from the archaeological record. Strepsiades, the protagonist of *Clouds*, in trying to persuade Socrates of his son Pheidippides's cleverness, says that as a child in the household, Pheidippides "fashioned clay houses [and] boats . . . ." A similar function has been suggested for a wheeled clay boat model from the ancient Mesopotamian site Warka,[13] found in a child's grave, and similar boat models are still made today as toys by children in Iraq.[14] The later reference is found in Plutarch's *Lysander* (XVIII.1). According to Plutarch, the Persian Cyrus gave a chryselephantine *trieres* 2 cubits long to the Spartan leader Lysander as a victory prize. The nature of the gift suggests that the model was the result of a naval confrontation, possibly the battle at Notion in 407 B.C. or the battle at the Aegospotami in 405 B.C. However, the point in Plutarch's narrative at which the model is mentioned suggests that the model was given to Lysander for his part in the final capitulation of Athens to Sparta in 404 B.C., in which warships were not a factor. The length and materials of the *trieres* model indicate that it was an actual warship replica rather than a rhyton or drinking vessel with naval attributes. The use of the model as an expensive gift is a new use for models and is otherwise unknown in ancient Greece. According to Plutarch, Lysander deposited Cyrus's gift at the treasury of the Acanthians at Delphi, along with a large amount of silver specie. Whether the model served as a votive, as a symbol of Lysander's celebrated aversion to personal wealth,[15] or as a symbolic adherence to the Spartan ban on privately held wealth is unknown.

For the Hellenistic period, a single reference to ship models is made by Diodorus Siculus in *Bibliothekes Historikes* (XVII.115.1–2). According to that author, Alexander the Great constructed a gigantic funeral pyre in the form of a square 1 stadion on a side to honor his dead companion Hephaestion. The exterior foundation walls were decorated with 240 golden (gilded?) *penteres* prows, on each of which were placed a pair of archers 4 cubits high and a single armed man 5 cubits high. The life-sized or greater scale of the warrior figures suggests a similar scale for the prows. Although Hephaestion's pyre, presumably synthesized from Egyptian and Near Eastern monumental architecture, is unrivaled in size and decoration by any contemporary or later funerary monuments, its most unusual features are the golden prows themselves. Neither Alexander nor Hephaestion were particularly inclined toward naval matters; the only war fleet Alexander had ever amassed was dismissed prior to his siege of Tyre, where it might have significantly helped his strategy. At least in scale, Hephaestion's pyre may have served as a model for later Hellenistic and Roman Imperial funerary monuments, as well as for the Roman *rostrum*. Hell. 9 and 12, marble funerary monuments from Rhenia and Rhodes, respectively, may also preserve faint echoes of Hephaestion's pyre.

Additional sources from the Roman Imperial and Byzantine periods further document ancient boat models. For instance, in Petronius's *Satyricon* (30), as Encolpius enters his host Trimalchio's dining room, he sees on the doorpost inscribed bronze *fasces*, finished "quasi embolum navis" ("like the ram of a ship"). Displayed so prominently, the *fasces* remind the guests of Trimalchio's magistracy,[16] and the warship ram is presumably an allusion to Trimalchio's earlier vocation as a shipping magnate, described in graphic detail in *Satyricon* (76). Elsewhere, in *Satyricon* (71), Trimalchio again refers to his shipping background, by requesting that his tomb be decorated with "naves . . . plenis velis euntes" ("ships . . . under full sail"). This reference, combined with Diodorus's description of Hephaestion's funeral pyre, suggests that large-scale funerary monuments with nautical iconography may have been more common than the archaeological record indicates and that the type may have carried over from the Hellenistic period into Roman Imperial times.

Also carried over from the Hellenistic period into Roman Imperial times were secular monuments of three-dimensional ships or portions of ships. A second century A.C. inscription from a bath building at Civita Lavinia refers to a "bronze basin with three waterspouts in the form of ships' prows," suggesting that a topical fountain decoration was included in the bathing complex. This sort of ship-fountain probably originated at Samothrace with the Nike fountain (Hell. 6).[17] The Byzantine historiographer Pseudo-Codinus mentions a similar sculpture at the Hippodrome in Constantinople—a "group of statuary, which includes a ship, representing, according to some, Scylla, who is eating the men from the whirlpool of Charybdis"[18]—possibly derived from the comparable group in the Sperlonga sculpture grotto (Hell. 7).

Athenaeus, writing in the late second to early third centuries A.C., supplies evidence that rhytons and household vases in the form of watercraft continued to be manufactured in his time. In *Deipnosophistae* (XI–XII), he names and defines several sorts of cups and other vessels. He uses some names interchangeably for boats and for cups that may have been boat-shaped. For example, Athenaeus (474b) uses the name *kantharos* both for a wine cup and for a warship with 20 oars. In light of Athenaeus's definition, Arch. 20, which combines warship attributes with characteristic features of both a *kyathos* and a *kantharos*, might more properly be classified as the latter. In the same section (474f), Athenaeus says that Asklepiades of Myrlea derived the *karchesion* cup type from the mast truck of a ship, which can also be cup-shaped.[19] Later, in describing the rhyton (sections 497b and 500f), Athenaeus quotes a few verses from a lost work by the second century B.C. poet Epinikos, who mentions a large rhyton, called a *trieres*, capable of holding a full *choa*. The *trieres* is again mentioned by Athenaeus (500e), in connection with a catalog of the household goods of a wealthy bridegroom. Similarly, Athenaeus (481f and 482d) associates the *kymbe* with both cups and boats, citing the grammarian Didymos and Sophocles's *Andromeda*, respectively. Athenaeus's association is reinforced by Apuleius in *Metamorphoses* (XI.269.4), in which Isis, goddess of navigation, appears in a vision holding in her left hand a golden *cymbium*.[20] This object, probably a boat-shaped lamp, served as one of Isis's maritime attributes. A number of ship-lamps from the Roman Imperial period incorporate Isiac and Serapian iconography.[21] In *Metamorphoses* (XI.16), Apuleius also discusses a Roman holiday, *Navigium Isidis*, which took place in March when followers of Isis launched a model ship into the sea. The vessel's sail was embroidered with the words "expressing wishes for the successful resumption of sailing." Several terracotta ship models that have been found in the waters off Greece and Cyprus were perhaps launched during this ceremony or an earlier, similar one.[22]

II

Representations of Ship and Boat Models

Unlike actual models, representations of ship and boat models are rare in Greek art. Only one example is known from the Bronze Age: the crescent-shaped boat borne by the foremost offering bearer in the presentation scene on the Late Minoan IIIA sarcophagus from Hagia Triada (Rep. 1). This model appears to represent an offering of some sort; however, whether it is a burial offering or a votive depends upon how the individual to the far right in the scene is interpreted.[1]

Following a hiatus of several hundred years, the next depictions of models after the Bronze Age are upon a group of four late Archaic Attic skyphoi (Rep. 2–5).[2] The models are small wheeled warship-carts in which are seated Dionysos, grasping a vine, and two flute players flanking him on either side. The scale of these models is shown by the small number of occupants, who fill the available space within the hull. In all cases, these late Archaic models are adorned at their sterns and along their hulls by drapery, which presumably served some ritual function in the Dionysiac procession.[3] Aside from the wheels below the hulls and the drapery, which covers the hulls down to the wheel hubs, Rep. 2–5 are indistinguishable from other contemporary depictions of full-scale single-level warships.

Rep. 6 and 6A, from the first century B.C., are the latest illustrations of watercraft models in Greek antiquity. Like Rep. 2–5, they also depict wheeled ship-carts; however, their Egyptian proveniences, papyriform hulls, Egyptian-style canopies, and bow protomes apparently identify them as local Egyptian rather than pan-Hellenic craft.[4] Although too little of the scene is preserved to be certain, the presence of wheels and towing lines suggests that Rep. 6 and 6A form part of an Isiac procession.[5]

CATALOG

Rep. 1. Boat model in presentation scene, Hagia Triada sarcophagus.
Late Minoan IIIA
Votive or burial offering
Restored L: 25 cm
Heraklion, Heraklion Museum

Behn, 1927/28 (vol. II):115; (vol. XI):242; De Ridder, 1909:513–17; Dussaud, 1914:403; Göttlicher, 1978:62, no. 318, pl. 24; Gray, 1974:G19, no. C 40; *Long, 1974:24, 44–49, 78, pl. 6, fig. 17, pl. 19, fig. 52; Marinatos, 1933:173, no. 18, 180, 195, n. 1, 196, n. 1, 234; Nilsson, 1950:426–39; *Paribeni, 1908:6–86, pl. 1.

Fresco with fragmentary boat model borne by foremost of three offering bearers. Restored at one end. Preserved end curves upward strongly to a point. Boat has curved or rocker bottom, rare in Bronze Age boat models. Along length of hull is a wide painted band, bounded on top and bottom by thin longitudinal lines. Between these are perpendicular alternating wide and thin lines, some wavy and some straight. These may represent either decoration, hull bindings, thwarts,[6] or frames.[7]

Rep. 1. Drawing by Vincent Amato, after Göttlicher, 1978.

Rep. 2. Wheeled warship-cart on Attic skyphos, from the Acropolis, Athens.

Ca. 500 B.C.

Vase painting

Dimensions unknown

Athens, Acropolis Museum 1281

Frickenhaus, 1912: supplement I, 1; *Graef and Langlotz, 1925:143, no. 1281, pl. 74; Haspels, 1936:250, no. 29; Moll, 1929: B VIb 117; Morrison and Williams, 1968:116, Arch. 101.

Fragmentary black-figure skyphos by the Theseus Painter (Morrison and Williams). Wheeled warship-cart in center of fragment; ram, portions of wheels, middle of sternpost missing; stern partially restored. Small bow compartment decorated with large oculus; leading edge of compartment marked by vertical stempost. Below oculus iris, ear and ruff of boar's-head ram are visible. Gunwale marked by zigzag line. Preserved tip of sternpost is canted, ending in two inward-curving terminals. Hull concealed by drapery to below level of wheel hubs. Drapery folds indicated by vertical incised lines, crossed by two horizontal painted lines. Stern decorated by irregularly shaped drapery, embellished with cross-hatching (restored). Dionysos seated in center of vessel, facing forward and holding grapevine in left hand. *Diaulos* player seated at trailing edge of bow compartment, facing aft; portions of other *diaulos* player are preserved in stern, facing forward.

Rep. 3. Wheeled warship-cart on Attic skyphos, from Akrai, Sicily.

Ca. 500 B.C.

Vase painting

H: 16.2 cm; W: 29.5 cm

London, British Museum B.79

Deubner, 1932:33–34, pl. 14.2; *Frickenhaus, 1912:supplement I, IIB; Haspels, 1936:250, no. 30; Morrison and Williams, 1968:116, Arch. 102.

Black-figure skyphos by the Theseus Painter (Morrison and Williams). Wheeled warship-cart in center of one side. Modern overpainting illustrated in Frickenhaus's work has been removed. Bow compartment missing. Below, ram is formed of pointed boar's head with articulated ear, eye, and jowls. Gunwale marked by two pairs of horizontal incised lines separated by black zone with overpainted

Rep. 3. Courtesy of the Trustees of the British Museum, London.

vertical chevrons. From lower pair of lines hangs drapery, covering lower portion of hull to below level of wheel axles. Drapery contains closely set vertical lines representing either folds or decoration. Stern concealed behind large rectangular drapery, decorated by diagonal cross-hatch pattern. Sternpost missing. Fragmentary Dionysos seated in center of vessel, facing forward and surrounded by fragments of grapevine. Lower body of another figure (*diaulos* player?) sits in stern, facing forward. Ship forms part of sacrificial procession.

Rep. 4. Wheeled warship-cart on Attic skyphos, from grave, Bologna.
Ca. 500 B.C.
Vase painting
H: 18 cm
Bologna, Museo Civico D. L. 109

Deubner, 1932:33–34; *Frickenhaus, 1912: supplements I, III; Haspels, 1936:253, no. 15; Laurinsich, n.d., vol. 2, p. 22, pl. 43; Moll, 1929: B VIb 116; Morrison and Williams, 1968:116, Arch. 103.

Black-figure skyphos by the Theseus Painter (Haspels). Surface slightly chipped. Wheeled warship-cart in center of one side. Vessel lacks stempost. Below, ram in form of boar's head with incised ear, eye, and mouth. Gunwale marked by two pairs of horizontal incised lines separated by black zone; at regular intervals along black zone are groups of three vertical incised lines, possibly depicting bindings or lashings of some sort. From lower pair of horizontal lines hangs drapery, covering lower portion of hull to level of wheel axles. Drapery decorated with diagonal incised lines. Stern also hung with large irregularly shaped drapery, decorated with diagonal cross-hatching. At stern, double sternposts rise in high curve from keel. Dionysos seated in center of vessel, facing forward and holding grapevine in left hand. Bearded satyr (?) stands at back of bow compartment, facing aft; behind Dionysos stands a *diaulos* player, facing forward. Ship forms part of sacrificial procession.

Rep. 5. Wheeled warship-cart on Attic skyphos fragment.

Ca. 500 B.C.

Vase painting

Dimensions unknown

Tübingen, Universität Tübingen 1497 (D 53)

Morrison and Williams, 1968:116, Arch. 104; *Watzinger, 1924:31, no. 53, inventory no. 1497, pl. 15.

Black-figure skyphos fragment, with short section of hull of wheeled warship-cart preserved. Right ear and eye and back portion of boar's-head ram preserved. Hull section comprises gunwale formed by two pairs of horizontal lines, with added white dots between each pair. From lower pair of lines, drapery hangs, decorated with wavy diagonal cross-hatch motif, filled in interstices with dot rosettes. Drapery conceals hull, hanging to level of wheel axle. Lower drapery hem is marked by pair of incised horizontal lines.

Rep. 6. Boat model on relief vase, from Egypt.

1st century B.C.

Vase decoration

Preserved W: 5 cm; preserved H: 6.2 cm

Athens, Benaki Museum 12775 (purchased in 1959 by Lucas Benaki)

E. Georgoula, personal communication, 18 June 1980; *Michaud, 1974:587, figs. 42–43.

Fragment of molded relief vase of light-colored clay, by the Memphis Workshop (E. Georgoula). Wheeled boat model in low relief forms part of a procession (Isiac?). Bow of boat not preserved. Hull is crescent shaped, with pair of oversized steering oars at stern, plied by helmsman. Single canopy slightly aft of amidships. Boat moves on pair of wheels. Behind, single individual pushes vessel at juncture between hull and wheels. Horizontal relief bands separate figured zone from decorated zones above and below: above, a repetitive dart motif; below, a floral zone under which is another zone decorated with upper portion of triangle motif. From same mold as Rep. 6A.

Rep. 6A. Boat model on relief vase, from Egypt.

1st century B.C.

Vase decoration

Preserved W: 8.9 cm; preserved H: 5.9 cm

Athens, Benaki Museum 12776 (purchased in 1959 by Lucas Benaki)

E. Georgoula, personal communication, 18 June 1980; *Michaud, 1974:587, figs. 42–43.

Fragment of molded relief vase of light-colored clay, by the Memphis Workshop (E. Georgoula). From same mold as Rep. 6, but additional details preserved in figured zone. Bow of crescent-hulled vessel has animal protome (horse?) facing forward; at bow are four men towing the vessel with thick lines.

Rep. 6A. Courtesy of the Benaki Museum, Athens.

III

Later Models in the Greek Tradition

Ship and boat models in the ancient Greek tradition continued to be produced long after the end of the Hellenistic period in 31 B.C. The primary center of production for these later models was the Italic peninsula, where models in the local tradition were produced from as early as the Villanovan Iron Age and models in the Greek style were manufactured in the Roman Republican period.[1] Although the Romans did not fight sea battles after the battle at Notion in 31 B.C., they continued to produce large amounts of naval iconography based upon the Greek paradigm in a variety of media.[2] For example, Roman lamps in the form of Greek-style warships were extremely popular quotidian objects and also votives, as inscribed examples have clearly demonstrated.[3] The Romans in the Imperial period also more fully developed the Hellenistic paradigms of small naval altars, fountains, and sundials with warship attributes.[4] Statue bases in the form of warships and statues with primary and secondary naval attributes, both of which originated in the Hellenistic period, were also popular in Imperial times.[5]

Probably the longest-lasting adaptations of the ancient Greek ship models are the Roman *rostrum* and commemorative columns.[6] These monuments, which appear to derive from Hellenistic monumental ship sculptures, were adorned by the Romans with either actual captured enemy warship prows or their simulacra and were erected in public forums throughout the Empire. Examples have been found in Italy at Rome, Ostia, and Aquileia and in the provinces in Germany, Spain, and England.[7] Postantique derivations of these monuments range in date from the Renaissance,[8] through the neoclassical period,[9] up to and including the modern era.[10]

Notes

1   INTRODUCTION

1. Qualls, 1980:12.

2. See Anonymous, 1978:189, no. 158 and figure.

3. See Landström, 1970:9ff.

4. See Landström, 1970:figs. 2, 19–29, 64–72.

5. See Reisner, 1913, and Landström, 1970.

6. Little aside from specialized excavation reports has been written concerning the later Egyptian models, of which some 15 examples have been published to date. See Göttlicher, 1978: 57–58, nos. 292–94, 297a, 298, p. 87, nos. 521–22; Weber, 1914:255–57, nos. 468–69, fig. 128, pl. 40, no. 269; Kaufmann, 1913:fig. 134, pl. 66, no. 673, inter alia.

7. See, for instance, Göttlicher, 1978:35, nos. 149, 151–52.

8. For the Cypriote firedogs, see the bibliography and notes for Geom. 2–5.

9. Some of the Cypriote models have not yet been published. For a selection of those that have, see Göttlicher, 1978:pls. 10–13, and Westerberg, 1983.

10. Karageorghis supports the hypothesis relating to transportation in the afterlife for the Cypriote models. See his articles listed in the bibliography, and the relevant discussion here in the chapter on the Geometric period.

11. The Sardinian models have yet to be systematically investigated. The primary sources for them to date are Lilliu, 1966, and Göttlicher, 1978:70–76, nos. 374–437, pls. 29–33. Neither source provides a complete catalog of examples.

12. The votive function is also documented on Populonia and on mainland Italy, where a number of the Sardinian models have been found. See Göttlicher, 1978:71–75, nos. 379, 421, 425, 427–28, p. 76, no. 433. See also D. Ridgway, in *JHS-AR* 20 (1973–74): 51.

13. See Göttlicher, 1978:77–79, nos. 444, 455, 459, 467; Edlund, 1980:22–23, 47, no. 26, pl. 10; Montelius, 1904 (vol. 2, part 2): pls. 257.15–257.17, 280.10; H. Hencken, "Tarquinia, Villanovans and Early Etruscans," *American School of Prehistoric Research, Peabody Museum, Harvard University Bulletin No. 23* (Cambridge, Mass.: Peabody Museum, 1968), p. 585, figs. 412b, 491a, 494b.

14. Reisner, 1913.

15. See Göttlicher and Werner, 1971.

16. See Göttlicher, 1978, reviewed by Johnston, 1979:6–7.

17. See Torr, 1964; Morrison and Williams, 1968; Bass, 1972; Casson, 1971; Gray, 1974.

18. See, for example, the photographs of BA 15 in the work of Laviosa, 1970, and of Hell. 6 in the work of Champoiseau, 1880.

2   BRONZE AGE

1. The evidence is in the form of Melian obsidian found in Mesolithic, and possibly even Upper Paleolithic, levels at Francthi Cave, on the Greek mainland. See Diamant, 1979:217, n. 24.

2. Representational evidence for water transport occurs earlier in Mesopotamia, in the fifth millenium B.C. See Qualls, 1980.

3. The earliest example from a secure mainland context dates to the Late Helladic IIIB–C periods (BA 20).

4. Greenhill, 1976:134 and fig. 83. Monozygous dugouts are normally rounded in section, reflecting the original form of the tree trunk from which they are fashioned.

5. Casson, 1971:8; Greenhill, 1976:134–41.

6. See Gray, 1974:fig. 3, for a compilation of "frying pan" boats.

7. Bass, 1972:20.

8. This conclusion assumes that the fish faces in the direction of travel. See Casson, 1959:41; 1971:41, n. 3; Hutchinson, 1962:92; Renfrew, 1972:356; Tsountas, 1899:90–91; Evans, 1928 (vol. II, part 1):241, n. 1; Behn, 1927/28:240; Cohen, 1938:489; Bass, 1972:17.

9. Both Renfrew, 1967:5, and Casson, 1971:41, state that the lead models from Naxos "prove" that the high end of the "frying pan" boats is the prow. However, Renfrew's own published drawing of BA 3 (Renfrew, 1972:358, fig. 17.7) clearly shows that there is no significant difference in height between the two ends.

10. Johnstone, 1973:9, notes that for the lead models from Naxos the angle of bow and stern to the bottom varies from 21 to 35 degrees, while on the "frying pan" boats the angle is 70 degrees. Thus, the angles on the engraved longboats are from two to three times greater than those on the lead models.

11. Doumas, 1968:285, suggests that there may have been added details in other materials which have since disappeared. Courbin, 1956:172, advances the same theory for Geom. 2 and 3, the firedogs from Argos.

12. Bass, 1972:17; Johnstone, 1973:6; Renfrew, 1972:357; Herbig: 1940:62.

13. For BA 8 the angle between the high end and the bottom is 65 degrees, which is close to the 70-degree angle for the engraved "frying pan" boats. See Johnstone, 1973:9.

14. Similarities between the Cycladic lead models and BA 8 are fewer, comprising only the low angular profile, the flat bottom, and one pointed and one blunted end.

15. Marinatos, 1933:217; Hutchinson, 1962:92; and Gray, 1974:G34, suggest that BA 8 represents a large vessel, not a small craft.

16. The minimum length for a craft with 12 men per side would be approximately 15 meters, allowing 1 meter of space per man and some additional room at bow and stern. Correspondingly, a Cycladic longboat with 26 men per side would have a minimum length of 30 meters, and probably more. This would approach in size the largest primitive wooden watercraft ever reported: a Tahitian war canoe of

108 feet (length overall 32.92 meters) recorded by Captain Cook. See Dodd, 1972:140–42.

17. Evans, 1921–1935 (vol. II):240; Bosanquet and Dawkins, 1923:7. Casson, 1971:41, n. 3, notes that "the horizontal extension still needs explaining . . . little is to be gained by guessing," thereby sidestepping the problem altogether.

18. Herbig, 1940:62; Köster, 1923, as cited by Marinatos, 1933:183; Marinatos, 1933:212; Stillwell, 1952:196.

19. Gray, 1974:G34; Köster, 1923:59.

20. Landström, 1961:27.

21. Betts, 1973:326.

22. Doumas, 1970/71:289; Johnstone, 1973:10.

23. Cohen, 1938:489.

24. Marinatos, 1933:183, n. 1.

25. As for instance in Polynesia, India, Oceania, and England. For bluff-bowed primitive vessels, see Hornell, 1946:pl. XXVII.A; Haddon and Hornell, 1937 (vol. I):219, fig. 148; 1937 (vol. II):16, fig. 16, p. 24, fig. 14, pp. 36–37, figs. 22–23, pp. 186–88, figs. 113–14, p. 304, fig. 171 (foreground); Hornell, 1920:176, fig. 21. Hornell, 1933:pl. 3, illustrates a Madura coaster with blunt prow and an ostensibly decorative ramlike keel projection at the bow, almost exactly like BA 8. However, the bow of the Madura craft is higher than the stern. For bluff-bowed dugouts from England, see McGrail, 1977:115–35.

26. See Morrison and Williams, 1968:pl. 1b.

27. Bass, 1972:17; Behn, 1927/28:240; Casson, 1959:41; 1971:41, n. 3; Cohen, 1938:489; Evans, 1921–35 (vol. II):241, n. 1; Hutchinson, 1962:92; Renfrew, 1972:356; Tsountas, 1899:90–91.

28. Johnstone, 1973:9, citing Sakellarakis, 1971:210. Reexcavation of the area where the pyxis was found has revealed additional fragments (P. Muhly, personal communication).

29. Casson, 1971:344. See the animal head ensigns on the Miniature Fresco from Thera, shown by Marinatos, 1974:colorplate 9.

30. In Egypt, the period most closely corresponding to the Early Bronze Age in Greece lasts from the later Thinite period to the Fifth Dynasty. See Landström, 1970:9, who bases his chronology on T. Säve-Söderbergh, *Egyptisk egenart* (Halmstead, 1968), pp. 117ff.

31. Landström, 1970:16.

32. Landström, 1970:32, 35–36, 39, and 42; Göttlicher and Werner, 1971:pl. 2, figs. 4(?) and 6, pl. 3, figs. 3–5 and 7. See, however, Göttlicher and Werner, 1971:pl. 2, figs. 3 and 8, pl. 3, fig. 8, where the opposite is true.

33. Bass, 1972:27, figs. 6–7, and Landström, 1970:figs. 17 and 22. Bass apparently missed the steering oar on his figure 6, although he does note that the ship is darker in color "to emphasize its individuality," and that it is a "foreign vessel."

34. However, the larger planked boats normally retain the form of a simpler dugout.

35. Dodd, 1972:frontispiece, 69 bottom, 70, 71 top and bottom, 85 top, 86–88, 89 bottom, 94–95, 97–98, 129–33, 136, 139, 142.

36. Dodd, 1972:frontispiece, 70, 71 top, 85 top, 86–88, 89 bottom, 94–95, 97–98, 129–33, 136, 139.

37. One New Zealand vessel in particular almost exactly duplicates the typical Early Cycladic longboat detail for detail: it has a high stern with two tassels attached at the top, an angular profile with the stern at a steeper angle to the keel than the low bow, a bow projection, and 22 paddlers along each side. See Dodd, 1972:71

top, after J. Hawkesworth, *Accounts of the Voyages . . . of Byron, Wallis, Carteret and Cook* (1773).

38. For a brief account of the validity of ethnographic analogy, see J. M. Coles, "Experimental Archaeology: Theory and Principles," in the work of McGrail, 1977:237.

39. Bifid and even trifid terminals are common features on ships on Cretan seals. See Marinatos, 1933:pls. XV–XVII; Cohen, 1938:figs. 6–7; Betts, 1973.

40. Marinatos, 1933:215.

41. Basch, 1975:201; Bass, 1972:17; Behn, 1927/28:241; Cohen, 1938:487; Fimmen, 1924:117, n. 3; Göttlicher, 1978:61, no. 313; Seager, 1909:290; Marinatos and Hirmer, 1976:pl. 10, caption.

42. See Doumas, 1968:285–90, for the hypothesis that BA 3–6 had added details in perishable materials. See Qualls, 1980:nos. 89, 91–92, for models from the Royal Cemetery of Ur, on which thwart notches have been cut, but the thwarts have not survived.

43. See Dodd, 1972, especially p. 135 for an outrigger attached to projecting stanchions. See also Haddon and Hornell, 1936 (vol. I):244, fig. 172, p. 333, fig. 244, p. 410, fig. 297, p. 435, fig. 312; 1937 (vol. II):295, fig. 171a.

44. Ca. 2113–2006 B.C. Qualls, 1980:nos. 47–48.

45. Ca. 2900–2750 B.C. Qualls, 1980:no. 221.

46. Dodd, 1972:69 top, 75, 76 top, 78–79, 96, 116, 135, 143–45, 148, 150; Greenhill, 1976:figs. 24, 46–47, 77–78, 80, 82, 84–86, 98, 100, 105; Hornell, 1946:figs. 20, 25, 27 (a bark canoe with projecting "feet" at both ends at level of waterline), 58, 60–62, 64, pls. VA–C, VIIA, XXVIA, XXXII–XXXIIIA, XXXVIIB, XLIA; Brøgger and Shetelig, 1951, 1971:37.

47. See Greenhill, 1976:36 and fig. 3.

48. Greenhill, 1976:fig. 99; Hornell, 1946:fig. 24; Brøgger and Shetelig, 1951, 1971:27–34.

49. Greenhill, 1976:143, fig. 97; Hornell, 1946:210, fig. 39. Both examples are single outrigger dugout canoes, on which the projecting forefeet extend horizontally, like BA 2. These features appear to serve either as cutwaters or as bow protectors.

50. See Brøgger and Shetelig, 1951, 1971; Greenhill, 1976.

51. It is assumed that BA 3–6 are from the same cist grave on Naxos. See Renfrew, 1967:5, 18.

52. Renfrew, 1972:431. For later periods, see Boardman, 1971:5–8; Kurtz and Boardman, 1971:207–8; Courbin, 1957:322ff. BA 1, 2, 7, and 8 are made of clay, which would eliminate any possible hypothesis concerning their intrinsic worth. However, BA 3–6 are made of lead, which was comparatively rare during the Early Bronze Age.

53. Evans, 1921–35 (vol. II):438–41; Schachermeyr, 1964:172; Boardman, 1971:7; Deonna, 1959b:247; Courbin, 1957:55–57, 63, 65.

54. Seager, 1909:290.

55. Renfrew, 1972:419–27, pls. 18, 4–5, and 23, 4a–b.

56. Renfrew, 1972:419, from Mochlos.

57. Alexiou, 1960:225ff.

58. Renfrew, 1972:431.

59. Renfrew, 1972:431; Long, 1974:44–49; Deonna, 1959a:247–53.

60. Ca. 2420–2270 B.C. See Reisner, 1913:I–IV.

61. Ca. 2650–2000 B.C. See Wooley, 1934:145–46 and pl. 19, in reference to the bitumen boat models from the Royal Cemetery at Ur, which Wooley thought had been manufactured on the spot specifically for placement in graves. Some models

were found with pottery inside, which was filled with foodstuffs presumably for use by the decedent en route to or in the afterlife.

62. See, however, Nilsson, 1950:623–30, who, following Paribeni, attempts to connect the boat depicted upon the Late Minoan Hagia Triada sarcophagus (Rep. 1, in Appendix II) with Egyptian funerary practices, stating that the boat would have been used by the apotheosized deceased to travel to Elysium, or the Isles of the Blest. See Long, 1974:48–49, for an alternate view.

63. See Levi, 1979 (vol. I):478, n. 170.

64. Renfrew, 1972:431–32.

65. Nilsson, 1950:56–57.

66. Nilsson, 1950:69–106. Included among the latter are terracotta locks of human hair. During the Roman period, genuine human hair was a specific maritime votive. See Lewis, 1958:110, no. 237.

67. Nilsson, 1950:68–108.

68. Nilsson, 1950:110, 122.

69. The Mochlos ring boat, with its striated hull and canopy, resembles Egyptian ships more than Aegean craft.

70. Nilsson, 1950:398.

71. Nilsson, 1950:398.

72. See the chapter on the Archaic period, below, for evidence for a patron deity for mariners.

73. See the catalog entries for BA 9–12.

74. See chapter 3.

75. For Mycenaean ship and boat representations, see Laviosa, 1969–70.

76. See Gray, 1974:figs. 6–9.

77. Pylos (An 657, An 654, An 519, An 656, and An 661).

78. See Chadwick, 1976:67, 175.

79. Chadwick, 1976:67.

80. Pylos (An 1). See Chadwick, 1976:173.

81. With one possible exception: the "ship" or "temple" bronzes mentioned on Pylos (Jn 829). The translation is uncertain. See Chadwick, 1976:141.

82. E. Vermeule, 1972:258.

83. See Bass, 1967:165–67, for a full discussion of the topic, and its arguments.

84. Caskey, 1964b:328.

85. Marinatos, 1933:174, 195.

86. Gray, 1974:G46; Laviosa, 1969–70:27; Marinatos, 1933:174.

87. Laviosa, 1969–70:27. The only visible projection evident in published photographs of BA 15 is at the bow, in which case it could not be a steering oar tiller.

88. On the Enkomi ships, the decks are so high that men stand below-decks, and both have masts stepped on the keel (keelson?) and passing through the deck unsupported.

89. Laviosa, 1969–70:27. Karageorghis, 1958:387, n. 4, compares the latter to the Arkesilas vase ships, also rendered in profile.

90. As Gray, 1974:G18; Marinatos, 1933:174; and Kirk, 1949:139, n. 58, assert.

91. See, however, Laviosa, 1969–70:27, who proposes a Late Minoan IIIC date.

92. It is possible that BA 17 and 23 are part of the same bronze model.

93. Petrakos, 1974:98–99.

94. As Petrakos, 1974:98–99, thought.

95. See the above examples (BA 18 and 25) and BA 21 and 24 for its presence on other models.

96. Cohen 1938:486ff.

97. Laviosa, 1969–70:17, figs. 8–9.

98. Cohen, 1938:486ff.

99. See E. Linder, "Naval Warfare in the El-Amarna Age," in the work of Blackman, 1973:317–24.

100. Casson, 1971:35, n. 13, citing Hornell, 1946:210.

101. Cohen, 1938:493.

102. See Frost, 1975:219–28.

103. Marinatos, 1974:colorplate 9, bottom, right of center.

104. Two of the small craft have only one man aboard at what corresponds to the helmsman's position, and three are unmanned; for these five, no means of propulsion is depicted, unless the "helmsmen" are punters.

105. Kirk, 1949:132.

106. A. N. Stillwell, 1952:196; Bosanquet and Welch, in the work of Atkinson, 1904:206; Cook, in the work of Whibley, 1931:568; Köster, 1923:24, n. 3; C. H. Smith, 1896–97:22. Smith, the original excavator, makes a strong case for the vessel's representing a skin boat, citing the ancient literary sources on the subject, the lack of wood in the Cyclades, and ethnographic analogies.

107. See, for instance, Marstrander, 1976:15, fig. 4.

108. Thus, see Hornell, 1946:figs. 13–14, 18–20, 22–23, 25–27, and pls. XXIII, XXIVB, and XXV.

109. Renfrew, 1967:5, 17–18; M. Warhurst, Keeper of Collections, Merseyside County Council, personal communication, 20 June 1980.

110. Marinatos, 1933:174.

111. Casson, 1975:10, n. 17.

112. Long, 1974:48.

113. Orlandos, 1970–71: 177.

114. Long, 1974:48.

115. Van Effenterre, 1969:103.

116. Long, 1974:48.

117. Mosso, n.d.:278.

118. According to Marinatos, 1933:217, n. 1, the hole may have been for fastening the steering oar (?).

119. Laviosa, 1969–70:27.

120. Schachermeyr, 1964:172.

121. Laviosa, 1969–70:26. This might be a rudimentary oculus.

122. Broneer, 1939:408.

123. Tamvaki, 1973:256.

124. In the available literature, two numbers are associated with this piece: KA 198–55, which may be a photograph number, and K3.600, which is also the inventory number for BA 17.

125. The descriptions of both Long and Göttlicher refer to BA 17, although Long, pl. 24, illustrates BA 24.

3   GEOMETRIC PERIOD

1. See, however, Brock, 1957:41–42, who states that the boat was found in a disturbed area. Brock later states (on p. 143) that the model and other objects from Tomb X "probably belong to this [i.e., the Protogeometric] period."

2. Morrison and Williams, 1968:12. Only three ships, of which two are on the

same vase, are dated to the Protogeometric period. See Gray, 1974:figs. 16a–b. The vase with the pair of ships is also from Crete; however, the ships bear little resemblance to Geom. 1. With some few exceptions, most of the remaining Geometric ship representations are of the Late Geometric period.

3. Geom. 2–4 and 6. Morrison and Williams, 1968:pls. 1a–c.

4. Morrison and Williams, 1968:pls. 1e, 2c, 3b, 4c–e, 5–6, and 7d.

5. Upward: Morrison and Williams, 1968:pls. 1e, 3b, 4e, 5, 6b, 6e, and 7d. Straight: ibid, pls. 4c, 6c–e.

6. Morrison and Williams, 1968:pls. 2c–d, 6b.

7. With the possible exceptions of Geom. 7 and 8 on, which have not yet been published.

8. The cheniskos is most prevalent during the following period; see Morrison and Williams, 1968:pls. 11a, 11d, 13, 14a, 14b, 14g, 15, 16c, 17a, 17c–e, 18a–b, 21d.

9. As does Casson, 1971:49.

10. Casson, 1971:fig. 68; Morrison and Williams, 1968:pls. 2b, 4a, and 6e.

11. The starboard side is flat and not meant to be seen.

12. Casson, 1971:50.

13. Homer, *Iliad* 1.309; Homer, *Odyssey* 1.280 and 4.669, as cited by Casson, 1971:44, n. 7.

14. Katzev, 1980:6 and figures.

15. None of the published photographs of Geom. 1 illustrate the port side interior.

16. There is, however, no evidence on the hull's interior for a mast step.

17. Brock, 1957:53, suggests that Geom. 1 was a toy.

18. Transom sterns are now thought to be a Hellenistic development. See Bonino, 1963:302–3; Casson, 1964:176; and Marsden, 1963:143–44, for a discussion of the origins of the transom stern.

19. London, British Museum C. 261, in the work of Walters, 1912:49, fig. 84.

20. Morrison and Williams, 1968:17.

21. Brock, 1957:43, citing Blegen, 1937:256.

22. Kouklia: Karageorghis, 1963b:277, 292–94, figs. 17–19; Patriki: Karageorghis, 1972:170–71, fig. 12.16, pl. XXXI.1; Salamis: Karageorghis, 1969:91ff., pls. 51–52.

23. Boardman, 1971:5–8; Courbin, 1957:384; and reply by Deonna, 1959b:252–53. A corollary of this hypothesis is that the firedogs were perhaps from the mess kits of sailors or marines. This would explain their shape as a souvenir of the decedent's profession.

24. Karageorghis, 1963b:293, and Deonna, 1959b:247–52.

25. Boardman, 1971:5–8, following Courbin, 1957:384.

26. Boardman, 1971:8; Karageorghis, 1963b:292–93.

27. Deonna, 1959b:252.

28. Boardman, 1961:132–33.

4   ARCHAIC PERIOD

1. This statement does not include Arch. 26–28 and 36–44, which are unpublished.

2. Representations of merchant vessels are extremely rare during the Archaic

period. See Morrison and Williams, 1968:pls. 9b, 9c, and 19, for the only other examples. Four models of merchant vessels of the Archaic period are known from Amathus on Cyprus.

3. Ohly, 1953:126, attributes an indeterminate number of these holes to tree roots.

4. Arch. 13, one of the best preserved, has a length-to-beam ratio of slightly more than 20:1.

5. Casson, 1971:82. Casson's ratio is reversed, and should read 1:10. Morrison and Williams propose a length-to-beam ratio of 7:1.

6. Morrison and Williams, 1968:pls. 1–7.

7. Ohly, 1953:112–13; Coldstream, 1968:321, 330. Buschor, 1937:204, offers a date in the mid seventh century B.C. for Arch. 10.

8. Ohly, 1953:118; Göttlicher, 1978:66, no. 325.

9. Göttlicher, 1978:64–66, provides dates for these ships ranging between 700 B.C. and the sixth century, without any explanation of his dating criteria. See Kyrieleis, 1980:87–88, for the chronology of Arch. 15–24.

10. Morrison and Williams, 1968:pls. 1–8.

11. Morrison and Williams, 1968:18–22, 25, 31, 34–38; Casson, 1971:64.

12. Morrison and Williams, 1968:pl. 4e.

13. Morrison and Williams, 1968:34, Geom. 33. Kirk, 1949:132, considered this feature a hawsehole for the anchor cable.

14. Morrison and Williams, 1968:74, Arch. 5, pl. 9a and 9c.

15. The Early Protoattic krater in Toronto; see Morrison and Williams, 1968:pl. 7d.

16. Morrison and Williams, 1968:pl. 10 and the following plates. It did not, however, completely replace the bow compartment oculus, as seen in the work of Morrison and Williams, 1968:pls. 15b and 20d.

17. Kirk, 1951:339, 342.

18. Morrison and Williams, 1968:82.

19. Kirk, 1951:341.

20. No ancient shipwreck is preserved to the deck level, and thus one cannot ascertain whether a similar practice was carried out in antiquity.

21. Kirk, 1951:340, and Morrison and Williams, 1968:82, suggest that the shape of the sternpost was dictated by the need for the spout at this place.

22. See Morrison and Williams, 1968:pls. 11–21, for this feature on contemporary paintings and reliefs.

23. See Eisman, 1971, plates.

24. See, for instance, Morrison and Williams, 1968:pl. 11 and the following plates.

25. For Egyptian crewmen, see Casson, 1971:figs. 8 and 10; Reisner, 1913; Göttlicher and Werner, 1971. For the Cypriote model, see Walters, 1912:49, fig. 84 (British Museum C. 261). The only Aegean Bronze Age crewmen in any medium are the crews of the ships in the Miniature Fresco from Thera, for which see Marinatos, 1974, and a single crewman on a Cretan sealstone, for which see Sakellarakis and Sapouna-Sakellarakis, 1981:221 top.

26. Geom. 1, with a single occupant, possibly the helmsman; Geom. 6, with five rowers.

27. See Morrison and Williams, 1968:pls. 3, 4, and 7.

28. See Kirk, 1951:339, 342.

29. The role of the *auletes* is to keep the rowers' stroke synchronized with his flute, but in Arch. 48 none of the men are rowing.

30. Similar gestures by a pair of crewmen in the stern of a small two-banked warship on a Late Corinthian aryballos appear to direct the rowers to row in unison. See Morrison and Williams, 1968:90, Arch. 50, pl. 12f (Casson, 1971:fig. 83).

31. See Göttlicher, 1978:26, no. 356a, pl. 26.

32. A number of anomalous features of Arch. 49 render it suspect. See the appropriate catalog entry.

33. There is only a single example from the Hellenistic period: Hell. 7 from Sperlonga. There are four from the Graeco-Roman period in Egypt (Haifa, National Maritime Museum, unnumbered; Fouquet Collections, unnumbered (bronze); Fouquet Collections, no. 299; Frankfurt, Stadtisches Museum Liebighaus, unnumbered) and only five from the entire Roman period (Athens, National Archaeological Museum MP 1140; Jerusalem, Palestine Archaeological Museum 38.1535; Metz, Metz Museum, unnumbered; Trier, Landesmuseum 768; New York, Metropolitan Museum of Art, 77.7). There are also two examples from pre-Roman Italy (lost models from Ruvo(?) and Bari).

34. Bronze Age: London, British Museum C. 261; Paris, Louvre AM 972; Cypro-Archaic period: Nikosia, Cyprus Museum 1937/VI-8.3, 1967/T.104/5, 1946/XII-23/1; Beirut, Chollot Collection (two examples).

35. See Sams, 1977:108–15, for beer drinking vessels with similar spouts from Gordion.

36. Arch. 30 and 32 were found in "Boeotia" and may also have been used as burial offerings.

37. Littman, 1916:57; Gusmani, 1964:no. 30.

38. The small number of examples renders any statistical analysis meaningless, at least for the Geometric period.

39. Arch. 10. Buschor, 1937:204.

40. Kopcke, 1967:145. If so, the crewmen's individual shares must have been rather small.

41. Andrewes, 1956:44.

42. Andrewes, 1956:118.

43. Andrewes, 1956:118–23.

44. Herodotos, *The Histories* 4.152.

45. Kyrieleis, 1980:22–24.

46. Buschor, 1937:204, fig. 7; Kopcke, 1967:145.

47. Ohly, 1953:111–12; Kopcke, 1967:145.

48. It seems unlikely, for example, that a model manufactured as a toy or lamp at Corinth would be used as a votive at another nearby site, especially one that was controlled by the other, as Perachora was by Corinth. See R. Stroud, in the work of R. Stillwell, 1976:687–88.

49. Couchoud and Svoronos, 1921:288–89, fig. 1.

50. Couchoud and Svoronos, 1921:288–89. It seems possible that the nautical graffito was added at a later date. Couchoud and Svoronos further restore the base as placed at the north end of the Sanctuary of the Bulls, although the base and the sanctuary are dated to the end of the seventh century B.C. and 246 B.C., respectively. See Tarn, 1910:209–22.

51. Marcadé, 1946:151, n. 1. The inscription is discussed by Jeffery, 1961:291, 304, no. 3, who tentatively dates it to 620–600 B.C.

52. Couchoud and Svoronos, 1921:288–89.

53. See Casson, 1971:344–48 and figs. 125, 127, 129–31, 144, and 151. Figure 129 has a device on the bow of a ship, dated to the first century B.C.–A.C., which

may represent a Medusa. In any case, all of these devices postdate Arch. 53 by several hundred years.

54. Littman, 1916:56–57.

55. Littman, 1916:56–57.

56. Gusmani, 1964:21.

57. From the orientation of the decoration, Arch. 2 could not be a ram, as Boehlau and Schefold, 1941:90, thought.

58. Boehlau and Schefold, 1941:90.

59. See Buschor, 1937:204.

60. D. Ridgway, personal communication, 31 October 1980.

61. Morrison and Williams, 1968:84.

62. Kirk, 1951:339–43.

63. Kilinski, 1978:181–82, 191.

64. Kilinski, 1978:190.

65. Strictly speaking, the tail is that of a marine mammal and not a fish, since it is horizontally disposed.

66. According to R. Stroud, in the work of R. Stillwell, 1976:687–88, the finds from the Heraion are in the National Archaeological Museum in Athens.

67. Payne's photograph is ambiguous, showing the boat only from above.

68. A. N. Stillwell, 1952:196, n. 10.

69. Couchoud and Svoronos, 1921:288, state that the base is triangular and in the form of a ship's prow, yet their reconstruction of the Sanctuary of the Bulls shows that it is trapezoidal (their figure 1).

5   CLASSICAL PERIOD

1. See, for instance, Morrison and Williams, 1968, chapter 9, and Jordan, 1975, inter alia.

2. Morrison and Williams, 1968:170–79, catalog only 21 ship representations for the Classical period, although they catalog 109 for the Archaic period.

3. See Eiseman, 1979.

4. Morrison and Williams, 1968:169.

5. A two-masted merchant vessel of the mid fifth century B.C., from the Tomba della Nave in Tarquinia. See M. Moretti, 1961; Casson, 1963:108–11.

6. See Morrison and Williams, 1968:73–117.

7. Morrison and Williams, 1968:169.

8. See Morrison and Williams, 1968:pls. 8b, 8e, 9b, 9c, 10d, 11a, 14c, 16d, 17a, 17c, 17d, 18a, 18b, 18d, 19, and 21e.

9. Morrison and Williams, 1968:179; Lloyd, 1975:48, n. 25.

10. As Kennedy, 1976:162, has suggested.

11. Morrison and Williams, 1968:179.

12. See Göttlicher, 1978:pl. 27, no. 362, section B.

13. Morrison and Williams, 1968:179.

14. Morrison and Williams, 1968:179; Rhousopoulos, 1862:39. Stais, 1907:231, no. 7038, considered the lump to be the base for an iron hook by which the model was suspended.

15. Anonymous, 1965, unpaginated caption, attributes Clas. 3 to the "XIV" century B.C., which may be either a misprint (intending the "IV" century B.C.?) or a misjudgment. The model bears no resemblance to any of the Bronze Age models.

16. See the catalog entry for Clas. 4 for the restored portions.

17. See, for instance, Morrison and Williams, 1968:pls. 11–26.

18. Morrison and Williams, 1968:179, 280.

19. It would be extremely difficult for a warship to disengage its ram from an enemy's hull if it had penetrated too deeply, and it would also risk damage to the rammer's outriggers and rowers.

20. As did Aristophanes, *Frogs* 364, cited by Morrison and Williams, 1968:283–84, n. 24.

21. See the catalog entry for Clas. 2 and Basch, 1972:44–45, for the range of dates for Clas. 2.

22. See Perlsweig, 1963; Bailey, 1975:29–30; Howland, 1958.

23. Morrison and Williams, 1968:179.

24. Sixth century B.C.: Basch, 1972:44; Göttlicher, 1978:68, no. 362.

25. The Zankle types with ship prows begin in 489 B.C. See, for instance, Jenkins, 1972:fig. 147.

26. Also turtles, waterfowl, and crocodiles. See Plaoutine, 1941, plates, for a representative sample of Apulian plastic vases with marine iconography. Seen in profile, Clas. 4 closely resembles Apulian foot *askoi*.

27. Although Clas. 1 is unpublished, other contents of the bothros were published by Bernabò-Brea and Cavalier, 1979:90–91.

28. Morrison and Williams, 1968:179; Basch, 1972:44–45.

29. See the earlier discussion, and Morrison and Williams, 1968:179.

6   HELLENISTIC PERIOD

1. The Egyptian example appears to represent a local rather than pan-Hellenic tradition. See the discussion of Hell. 36 and its catalog entry.

2. This perspective is best shown by Felbermeyer, 1971:136.

3. See, for instance, the relief of an oared galley of ca. 200 B.C. from Lindos, Rhodes, in the work of Morrison and Williams, 1968:pl. 27d, reconstructed by Casson, 1971:fig. 108. See also Casson, 1971:figs. 109, 110, and 114, for a similar treatment on Roman warships.

4. Casson, 1971:226–27.

5. Casson, 1971:fig. 108.

6. See Casson, 1971:figs. 114, 129, 131, 146, 147, 149, 154–56, and 181.

7. The other is Hell. 36, on the upper deck of which are broken stubs of missing features.

8. Basch, 1975:207. Walters, 1903:336, no. D 201, considered the blades to be lotus flowers.

9. Walters, 1903:336, no. D 201. Although the ram tip is in the form of a lion's head, it is not clear from Walter's description or from photographs whether there is an actual spout connecting the ram and the rhyton's interior.

10. Basch, 1975:207ff.

11. For Roman rams with superimposed blades, see Basch, 1975:figs. 15A–D; Göttlicher, 1978:pls. 38 and 39.

12. If the wale terminals doubled as subsidiary rams, as some scholars have suggested, they might spring loose upon impact against an enemy's hull.

13. On Hell. 1, the bow compartment railing as restored wrongly cuts off the dolphin's tail. The overly liberal restoration may also account for the brevity of the uppermost wale.

14. See, however, the catalog entry for Hell. 1, which describes the other associated features on the back of the rhyton.

15. See Casson, 1971:fig. 74 (Morrison and Williams, 1968:28, Geom. 19, pl. 4e).

16. On the Aristonothos krater, shown by Morrison and Williams, 1968:74–75, Arch. 5, pl. 9c.

17. Morrison and Williams, 1968:86, Arch. 35, pl. 11d. Basch, 1966:118, considered the *aphlaston* shield to be a Roman warship element, originating with the Etruscans and later borrowed by the Greeks.

18. See Casson, 1971:fig. 108. It is also popular on Roman warships from the Republican period onward, for which see Basch, 1966; Casson, 1971:figs. 114, 119–21, 129, 131, 140, and 141.

19. Morrison and Williams, 1968:179, Clas. 29, include Hell. 35 in their catalog for the Classical period, although they state: "The date of this terracotta is uncertain, but possibly Hellenistic."

20. Köster, 1923:88.

21. De Graeve, 1978:243.

22. Morrison and Williams, 1968:49; Basch, 1968a:168.

23. Basch, 1968a:168–70.

24. Basch, 1968a:169, citing Assman, 1892:52–53.

25. See, for instance, Morrison and Williams, 1968:37, Geom. 43 and 44, pls. 7e and 7f; and ibid., pls. 8a, 10d, and 22a, for the Archaic period.

26. See Morrison and Williams, 1968:180, Hell. 1; Basch, 1969a:158–59, 232–34.

27. See Basch, 1968a.

28. Lloyd, 1975:47–48; Alexanderson, 1914:38.

29. Basch, 1969b:152–59. See also Casson, 1971:94–96. Basch hypothesizes that the model may have been a sailor's offering at the Bucheum at Erment, which dates from ca. 350 B.C. Elsewhere in the same article (pp. 234–35), Basch points out that after Alexander the Great conquered the Phoenician cities along the eastern coast of the Mediterranean in 332 B.C., those cities began producing ships on coin types with more "Greek" or "Graeco-Roman" than Phoenician naval architecture. The possible conclusion, therefore (not made by Basch), might be that Hell. 36 falls between the two dates, or ca. 350–332 B.C. However, it is unknown whether Hell. 36 was actually found at the Bucheum; according to Breitenstein, 1941:56, no. 520, the only provenience supplied by the seller (a Cairo dealer in 1902) was "Erment."

30. Casson, 1971:98.

31. Casson, 1971, chapter 6, devotes an entire chapter to a discussion of the invention, development, and propulsion of *polyereis*.

32. See Casson, 1971, chapter 6.

33. Blinkenberg, 1938; 1941; Casson, 1971:129–31, n. 116; Morrison, 1980:122.

34. For a full description of the dedicatory inscription, see Blinkenberg, 1941, who discusses all earlier bibliography as well.

35. According to Blinkenberg, 1938:40; 1941:301; and Marcadé, 1946:147, 151 (with bibliography), the two upper courses are *lithos larticos*.

36. Blinkenberg, 1938:40, citing Kinch, the excavator and reconstructor; Morrison, 1980:125; Basch, 1969b:437.

37. Morrison and Williams, 1968:284, claim that the closed area on which the Nike alights is the closed deck, or *katastroma*. However, this area would have to be solid to support the statue. It seems likelier that it simply represents the bow compartment.

38. According to Marcadé, 1946:146, n. 6, some (unspecified) fragments of Hell. 6 are still in Samothrace.

39. See Casson, 1971:119 and fig. 118, for a discussion and photograph of the oarports on Hell. 6. Casson believes that the oars were attached to the trailing edge of the tholepin by an oar strap. For further discussion and alternate views of the oarport and tholepin arrangement, see Thurneyssen, 1979, and Humphreys, 1978.

40. Blinkenberg, 1938:21–44; Morrison, 1980:125.

41. At one time, Morrison and Williams, 1968:286, considered Hell. 6 to be a *tetreres* or *penteres*; Casson, 1971:103, considered it a *penteres*. Morrison, 1980:125, changed his mind, and suggested that Hell. 6 represents a *trihemiolia*, following Blinkenberg.

42. The bows of the others are too badly preserved for one to determine whether they too had nozzles at the bow.

43. P. Bruneau, in the work of Stillwell, 1976:261–62.

44. Bruneau, 1965:107–8.

45. See catalog entries for Hell. 14–30 for proveniences. It would of course not be expected that any of the models would be found in funerary contexts, since all of the graves on Delos were moved to Rhenia by 426 B.C., and all subsequent burials were made on Rhenia. See Bruneau, 1965:261.

46. Only two examples are known from antiquity of ship-shaped sundials: the other is from Sparta and may date to the second century A.C. See Basch, 1969b:434–39, fig. 2, pl. IV; Gibbs, 1976: 89, 319–20, no. 3107G, with figures.

47. See Tarn, 1910:209–22; Couchoud and Svoronos, 1921:270–94.

48. Deonna, 1938:198–99, 339, pl. 3, nos. 28–35. Nautical imagery symbolic of hope and good luck is well known in Paleochristian iconography, but is not attested in Greek and Roman iconography. See Lehmann and Lehmann, 1973. Deonna, 1938:197, 199, fig. 234, pl. III, no. 21, also published a small (9 cm high) stamped lead warship pendant, possibly a votive or fishing weight, from an unknown provenience on Delos. He dated it for unknown reasons to the Republican period (Delos, Delos Museum A 3882). See also Hell. 37.

49. See Couilloud, 1974:nos. 337–59.

50. Cavvadias, 1891:39, supported by Lehmann and Lehmann, 1973:193, n. 16. See, however, Meiggs, 1966, for some of the problems relating to dating inscriptions solely on the basis of the letter forms.

51. Cavvadias, 1891:38; Göttlicher, 1978:68–69, no. 368; Woelcke, 1911:155. As Blinkenberg, 1938:32, n. 1, rightly states, there is no firm basis whatever for suggesting a Victory figure. The above opinions are based solely on the Nike of Samothrace, which is much later.

52. The base is visible in plate IX of Defrasse and Lechat, 1895, where it seems to be oriented toward the altar of the Asklepios temple.

53. Cavvadias, 1891:39, further suggests that the now missing statue may have been expropriated as booty by L. Mummius and replaced by a statue of himself.

54. That connection was left for the Romans. Around 100 B.C., in the later Republican period, a naval monument was erected by a victorious general on the Tiber Island at Rome, which was traditionally associated with Asklepios. See Lehmann and Lehmann, 1973:200–201; Besnier, 1902; Krauss, 1944; Rubin de Cervin, 1954; Le Gall, 1953:102ff. According to Lehmann and Lehmann, 1973:194, n. 18, Hell. 13 "is said to have been found in the Asklepion (of Kos) but its original context is unknown."

55. Only Lehmann and Lehmann, 1973:193, n. 17, have doubted the original location of Hell. 5, stating, "The fragments were discovered out of context of their

original position, and it is a mere conjecture that they were placed in the huge outer stoa of the sanctuary." However, it seems unlikely that both the base and its associated fragments would be moved from their original position; nor is there any mention that the present location of the monument differs from its ancient position in any of the published reports to date (see catalog entry for bibliography). See Blinkenberg, 1938:30; 1941:302, for the date of Hell. 5. Blinkenberg's chronological criterion revolves around the name of Agathostratos Poluartou as trierarch on the inscription on Hell. 5; in Polyainos *Stratagems* (5.18), mentions Agathostratos Poluartou as nauarch of the Rhodian fleet at the Battle of Ephesus in 258 B.C. Since the rank of nauarch is higher than that of trierarch, Blinkenberg assumes that Agathostratos Poluartou would have attained nauarch status a few years after being a trierarch. See also Marcadé, 1946:148.

56. For the complete (as preserved) inscription, see Blinkenberg, 1941. Blinkenberg, 1938:37, suggested that the monument might commemorate a victory by the Rhodians over pirates, of which the Tyrrhenians were the most active exponents during the period in question.

57. Blinkenberg, 1938:33.

58. Blinkenberg, 1938:33; 1941:305. Werner, 1970:figs. 4–6, published drawings of Hell. 5, of which the plan view shows a large round feature on the upper surface of the uppermost course. This feature is the right size and in the right position for the attachment point for a statue.

59. Blinkenberg, 1938:33; 1941:301.

60. Blinkenberg, 1938:37, citing Kinch; Lehmann, 1955:72; Morrison, 1980:125.

61. Morrison, 1980:125; Casson, 1971:102; Bieber, 1955:125–26; Basch, 1969b:437. As Bieber pointed out, in the early second century B.C. the Rhodians were allied with the Romans in a number of successful naval campaigns against the Syrians and Macedonians. See Thiersch, 1931:338ff., for a discussion of the fragmentary inscriptions associated with Hell. 6, and Lehmann and Lehmann, 1973:192, for an opposing view.

62. See Merker, 1973:6.

63. Hell. 6 also had rippled pavement slabs imitating water, as well as attachment holes in the pavement for other statues: possibly dolphins, according to Lehmann and Lehmann, 1973:184.

64. Lehmann, 1955:72.

65. Apparently, there were other marble ships' prows on Samothrace in antiquity: Morrison, 1941:23, refers to "several statue bases in the shape of prows found at Samothrace," and Lehmann and Lehmann, 1973:196, n. 22, citing Otto Kern, *RE* 10 (1919): column 1432, mentions a marble ship's prow seen in Samothrace "about 50 years ago," which is now missing. However, according to J. R. McCredie, personal communication, 26 August 1980, Hell. 6 is the only three-dimensional ship representation from Samothrace.

66. See the references cited in the catalog entry for Hell. 8. Neither the enclosure nor the base has been fully published to date. Lehmann and Lehmann, 1973:196, n. 25, dated Hell. 8 to the Roman period, on the basis of the crudity of the workmanship.

67. For the placement of Hell. 8, see Martin, 1959:plans A and B.

68. See Ermeti, 1981.

69. Goodchild, 1963:49.

70. Various hypotheses include a Nike of Benghazi (Deonna, 1938:193, n. 1), an Athena Nike (Caputo, 1968:233, citing Stucchi), the nymph Cyrene (Caputo), or possibly a generic Victory figure.

71. Säflund, 1972:20.

72. Lauter, 1969:169.

73. W. H. Gross, *Nachr. Giess. Hoch-Schulges* 35 (1966), cited by Lauter, 1969:162.

74. Felbermeyer, 1971:142. Felbermeyer's entire article may be ignored, if for no other reason than that he refers to the preserved portion of Hell. 7 as the bow of a ship.

75. von Blanckenhagen, 1976:102.

76. Athanodoros, Hagesandros, and Polydorus, whose names are inscribed on the base of Hell. 7 but in letter forms attributed to the Roman period. See von Blanckenhagen, 1976:101; Lauter, 1969:102, citing Jacopi.

77. Homer, *Odyssey* 12.234ff.; Ovid, *Metamorphoses* 13; Virgil, *Aeneid* 6.837ff. See von Blanckenhagen, 1976:102, for a discussion of the possible literary sources.

78. von Blanckenhagen, 1976:102–3, citing Conticello and Andreae, 1974.

79. See Conticello and Andreae, 1974.

80. See the references and dates in the catalog entry for Hell. 7.

81. My knowledge of this most unusual object is limited to a single passing reference made at the annual Archaeological Institute of America/American Philological Association meetings in Atlanta, Georgia, in December 1977, where it was erroneously referred to as a "trireme."

82. See Deonna, 1938:339, pl. III, nos. 28–35.

83. Blinkenberg, 1938:40, citing Kinch; Morrison, 1980:125; Bieber, 1955:125. According to Lehmann, 1955:72, the crowning Victory figure is of Parian marble.

84. See von Blanckenhagen, 1976:100; Lauter, 1969:172.

85. Göttlicher, 1978:69, after Reinach, 1912:311–12.

86. Gibbs, 1976:91.

87. Deonna, 1938:193.

88. Plassert, 1912:394.

89. Lehmann and Lehmann, 1973:194, n. 21, citing J. D. Kondis.

90. Other portions may be missing as well; this catalog description is based upon the only published photograph of this prow, by Lehmann and Lehmann, 1973, which shows only the starboard side.

91. See, for instance, the Roman prows from Ostia shown by Göttlicher, 1978:81, nos. 486–87, pl. 38.

92. Basch, 1968a:168–69.

93. Assman, 1892:52–53.

94. Basch, 1969a:232–34.

7   CONCLUSIONS

1. Although nearly as many (17) were found from Archaic Corinth.

2. It is also possible that the island bias reflects modern archaeological site selection, although this seems unlikely.

3. BA 10 and 11 and Geom. 7 are of unknown materials.

4. However, as is the case for the Classical period, the numbers from the Geometric period are so small as to be statistically useless.

5. During the American Revolutionary period, for example, when the British overbuilt their ships so that they could be used for both long-distance trade and warfare. See Johnston et al., 1978:220.

6. The latter figure does not include the 15 other models from Delos, all of

which were found scattered throughout the city, but which do not have specific proveniences.

7. See A. N. Stillwell, 1952.

I   WRITTEN SOURCES

1. Homolle, 1886:466, line 131.

2. Homolle, 1882:32, line 31, p. 116, n. 2; 1890:409, lines 76–83; 1903:91; Durrbach, 1926:60–68, no. 313, line 19; 1929:34–37, no. 385, line 60, pp. 98–103, no. 421, line 59, pp. 104–5, no. 423, line 5, pp. 113–15, no. 439, lines 29–30, pp. 128–76, no. 442, line 31, pp. 259–75, no. 461, line 39.

3. Homolle, 1882:116, n. 2.

4. Homolle, 1890:409, lines 76–83.

5. Durrbach and Roussel, 1935:114–21, no. 1432, Ab, col. 2, lines 55–56.

6. Durrbach, 1929:164.

7. Earlier references to ship models are found in Mesopotamian literature. See Göttlicher, 1978:13; Qualls, 1980.

8. Wilamowitz-Moellendorff, 1919:61.

9. Prokopios, *History of the Wars* 8.22, 23–27.

10. Marcadé, 1946:151.

11. W. Smith, 1880 (vol. II):1129; Lippold, in the work of Pauly-Wissowa, *RE* 16, no. 1 (1933): 1105.

12. See Lloyd, 1975:46, sec. 5 and n. 14, 52, sec. 5; *JEA* 58 (1972): 307–8, pl. XLVI.

13. Baghdad, Iraq Museum W 20 972, 1. See Lenzen, 1963/64:642, fig. 6.

14. See Ochsenschlager, 1974.

15. Plutarch, *Lysander* 2.4–5, 16.1.

16. Heseltine, 1956:434, n. 1.

17. Lehmann and Lehmann, 1973:203, n. 33, citing *NSc* 1881:139; Visconti, *BullComm* (1882):66ff.

18. Säflund, 1972:58, n. 56, citing *Script. or Const.* II, p. 190, 12ff.

19. See, for instance, Morrison and Williams, 1968:pls. 10d, 13, and 21e; Casson, 1971:fig. 144 right.

20. See Gwyn Griffiths, 1975:32, 75, 195–96, for a discussion of the boat-shaped lamp or cup of Isis.

21. See especially Walters, 1905:403, pl. LXIII, fig. 1; 1914:56, no. 391, figs. 65a–b, no. 392, figs. 66a–b, p. 31, no. 12, fig. 9, pls. 12a–b; Bruneau, 1974:339, fig. 2; Göttlicher, 1978:87, no. 529, pl. 42.

22. See Basch, 1968a:136–66, fig. 1, pl. I, and the following plates, and Westerberg, 1983:14, no. 8, figs. 8 and 16, no. 11, fig. 11. Because of the lack of provenience, these models are difficult to date. However, Westerberg's dates of the Late Cypriote period for the two Cypriote models are almost certainly too early.

II   REPRESENTATIONS OF MODELS

1. For the most recent and comprehensive discussion of the iconography of the Hagia Triada sarcophagus, see Long, 1974.

2. Arch. 105 of Morrison and Williams, 1968:116, may be a fifth example of this group of ship-carts.

3. For a discussion of the Dionysiac procession and its place in the Athenian calendar of festivals, see Frickenhaus, 1912, and Deubner, 1932:33–34.

4. The enumerated features are anachronisms from as early as the Bronze Age: see Landström, 1970:fig. 22 and the following figures.

5. Michaud, 1974:587–91.

6. Marinatos, 1933:173.

7. Long, 1974:48.

III   LATER MODELS IN GREEK TRADITION

1. See Le Gall, 1953:102ff.; Basch, 1966; von Gerkan, 1922:55–73.

2. See Casson, 1971:141ff.; Blinkenberg, 1938:40, n. 2.

3. See Walters, 1914:56, nos. 390–91; Seyrig, 1951:101–3; Weber, 1914:31, no. 12; Göttlicher, 1978:85, no. 507.

4. See Jones, 1912:327–31, nos. 26a–27a; Lehmann and Lehmann, 1973:200–204, 224–34, figs. 18, 20, 21, and 39–44; Göttlicher, 1978:81, nos. 486–87, pl. 38; Gibbs, 1976:89, 319–20, no. 3107G, with figures.

5. See Bruneau, 1974:365–70, 375–79, figs. 16–18; Anonymous, *AA* 50 (1935): 329–33, fig. 3; Lehmann and Lehmann, 1973:202–8, nn. 32, 37; Anonymous, *Fasti* 8 (1953): nos. 3181, 3630, fig. 85; Bianchi-Bandinelli, 1971:325, fig. 304; Le Gall, 1944:38–55, fig. 1; Göttlicher, 1978:83–87, nos. 494, 514, 520, pls. 39 and 41; Helbig, 1966:275–76, no. 367 (162), p. 415, no. 531; Basch, 1969b:430–33, fig. 1, pls. I–III, pp. 439–43, figs. 3, 5f, pls. Va and Vb; Lowrie, 1901:51–57, figs. 1 and 2; Franzoni, 1973:92–94, nos. 71–73; von Gerkan, 1922:55–73, figs. 66–87, pls. 2, 8–9, 11, 19–22, and 25–28.

6. Comparatively little modern study has been made of these unusual monuments. See Mau, 1905; Peterson, 1906; Scheel, 1928.

7. See Lehmann and Lehmann, 1973:206, n. 37; Göttlicher, 1978:81–85, nos. 482, 488–89, 497, 507, pls. 37–40.

8. The so-called "Duilius Monument," a rostral column in the Capitoline Museum in Rome. See Helbig, 1966:471–73, no. 1680.

9. During the French neoclassical period, a number of triumphal monuments with ancient naval iconography were designed but never erected. For Petitot's bridge design of ca. 1748 A.D., see Harris, 1967:195, pl. XX, 32; for Jardin's ship-bridge of the mid eighteenth century A.C., see Harris, 1970:pl. 16; for Ledoux's ship-bridge of 1773–79 A.D., see Anonymous, 1968:127, no. 78; for Boulée and Perronet's ship-bridge of the late eighteenth century A.C., see Anonymous, 1968:65, no. 38; for Mezzani's design for a triumphal arch of 1806 A.D., see Anonymous, 1978, cover illustration; for the commemorative rostral column erected between 1810 and 1816 A.D. by Thomas de Thomon in St. Petersburg, Russia, and the tomb of the navigator Dumont D'Urville, erected in the Parisian Montparnasse cemetery in the mid nineteenth century A.C., see Hautecoeur, 1955:250–52, fig. 217. The neoclassical period in England also produced some examples of monumental naval commemoratives with ancient naval iconography, such as the monument to Lord Collingwood of 1813 A.D. by Westmacott, and the monument to Admiral Lord Howe of 1803 A.D. by Flaxman. See Irwin, 1966:figs. 80 and 84.

10. See, for example, the Monument of Victor Emmanuel II in the Piazza di Venezia in Rome, dedicated in 1911 A.D., which includes warship rams in the ancient Greek tradition.

Glossary

Acrostolion. Sternpost

Aphlaston. Sternpost or its ornament

Aplustre. Sternpost ornament

Aryballos. Small rounded container for carrying scented oil or cosmetics

Askos (plural *askoi*). Small jug

Auletes. Flute player

Bothros. Pit, usually for burials

Cheniskos. Sternpost ornament in the form of a goose head

Choa. Small jug for holding various liquids, especially wine

Cymbium. Variant of *kymbe* (see below)

Diaulos. Double flute, played aboard ships to assist the rowers in synchronizing their strokes

Epotis (plural *epotides*). Forwardmost surface of the outrigger on a *trieres* (see below)

Fasces. Bundle of rods serving as a symbol of Roman authority

Kantharos. Small, single-handled cup, larger than a *kyathos* (see below)

Katastroma. Deck of a ship

Krater. Large vase for mixing and dispensing wine

Kyathos (plural *kyathoi*). Small, single-handled cup

Kymbe. Word for both a cup and a small craft

Lar. Roman household god

Lithos larticos. Type of stone from Rhodes used in the construction of buildings and monuments

Malagma. Fender or bumper used to prevent a ship from rubbing or bumping against a wharf or another vessel

Penteres. Warship developed in the fourth century B.C. in which a combination of single or multiple rowers in groups of five were distributed over one bank or more of oars

Polyereis. Large war galleys with up to three superimposed banks of rowers, some of which could employ more than one man per oar

Proembolon. Subsidiary ram at the prow of a warship

Protome. Head; in this context an animal head that could decorate the bow or stern of a ship

Pyxis. Small jug or container for cosmetics, etc.

Rostrum. Warship ram, often removed from a captured enemy vessel and attached to a commemorative victory monument; also, the victory monument itself

Skyphos. Small cup

Tetreres. War galley developed in the fourth century B.C. in which a combination of single or multiple rowers in groups of four were distributed over one bank or more of oars

Thyrsos. Vine- or ivy-covered staff associated with Bacchic ritual or celebration

Trieres. Warship with three banks of superimposed rowers

Trihemiolia (plural *trihemioliai*). Type of swift warship, possibly derived from the three-banked *trieres*

Bibliography

The abbreviations used in this bibliography are the standard abbreviations recommended by the *American Journal of Archaeology*, volume 82, 1978, pages 5–10.

Adamesteanu, D. "Uno scarico di fornace ellenistica a Gela." *ArchCl* 6 (1954): 129–32.

Alcock, J. P. "Celtic Water Cults in Roman Britain." *ArchJ* 122 (1965): 1–12.

Alexanderson, A. M. "Den Grekiska Trieren." *UppsÅrsskr* 1, no. 9.7 (1914): 38.

Alexiou, S. "E minoike thea meth'upsomenon xeiron." *KrChron* 12 (1958): 179–299.

———. "New Light on Minoan Dating: Early Minoan Tombs at Lebena." *ILN*, 6 August 1960, p. 225.

———. *Guide to the Archaeological Museum of Heraklion*. Athens: General Director of Antiquities and Restoration, 1968.

———. "Forschungsbericht zur ägäischen Fruhzeit." *AA* 86 (1971): 305–44.

———. Review of Gray, 1974. *AJA* 80 (1976): 205–6.

Anderson, R. C. *Oared Fighting Ships*. London, 1962.

———. "A Galley-Model in the Louvre." *Mariner's Mirror* 52 (1966): 370.

Andrewes, A. *The Greek Tyrants*. London: Hutchinson's University Library, 1956.

Anonymous. *Führer durch das Antiquarium*, vol. I. Berlin: de Gruyter, 1924–32.

———. "Chroniques des fouilles en 1949." *BCH* 74 (1950): 333–64.

———. *Cincinnati Art Museum Bulletin* 7 (1965).

———. *Guide de Thasos*. Paris: École française d'Athènes, 1967.

————. *Visionary Architects: Boulée, Ledoux, Lequeu.* Houston: University of St. Thomas, 1968.

————. *Der Garten in Eden.* Munich: Prähistorische Staatssamlung, 1978a.

————. *Venezia nell'eta di Canova 1780–1830.* Venice: Alfieri, 1978b.

Aristophanes. *The Clouds.* Translated by B. B. Rogers. London and Cambridge, Mass.: Heinemann and Harvard University Press, 1950.

Assman, E. "Nautisch-Archäologische Untersuchung." *JdI* 7 (1892): 42–53.

Aström, P. *The Middle Cypriote Bronze Age.* Lund: Ohlsson, 1957.

————. *Studies on the Arts and Crafts of the Late Cypriote Bronze Age.* Lund: Förf, 1967.

Atkinson, T. D., et al. "Excavations at Phylakopi in Melos." *JHS*, supplementary paper no. 4, 1904.

Bailey, D. M. *A Catalogue of the Lamps in the British Museum,* vol. I. London: British Museum, 1975.

Banti, L. "I culti minoici e greci di Hagia Triada (Creta)." *ASAtene* III–IV (1941–43): 9–74.

Barnett, R. D. "Early Shipping in the Near East." *Antiquity* 32 (1958): 220–30.

Basch, L. "A Model of an Ancient Warship in the Louvre." *Mariner's Mirror* 52 (1966): 115–26.

————. "Appendice. Le modèle de Corpus Christi College à Cambridge." *AntCl* 37 (1968a): 166–71.

————. "Un modèle de navire romain au Musée de Sparte." *AntCl* 37 (1968b): 136–71.

————. "Phoenician Oared Ships." *Mariner's Mirror* 55 (1969a): 139–62, 227–45.

————. "Trois modèles de navires en marbre au Musée de Sparte." *AntCl* 38 (1969b): 430–46.

————. "Ancient Wrecks and the Archaeology of Ships." *International Journal of Nautical Archaeology* 1 (1972): 1–58.

————. "Graffites navales à Délos." *BCH-Supp.* 1 (1973): 65–76.

————. "Another Punic Wreck in Sicily: Its Ram." *International Journal of Nautical Archaeology* 4, no. 1 (1975): 201–19.

————. "One Aspect of the Problems Which Arise from the Interpretation of Representations of Ancient Ships." *Mariner's Mirror* 62 (1976): 231–33.

Bass, G. F. "Cape Gelidonya. A Bronze Age Shipwreck." *TAPS* 57, no. 8 (1967): 1–177.

Bass, G. F., ed. *A History of Seafaring.* London: Thames and Hudson, 1972.

Bathe, B. W. *Ship Models: From the Earliest Times to 1700 AD.* London, 1966.

Beazley, J. D. *Attic Black-Figure Vase-Painters.* Oxford: Clarendon Press, 1956.

Behn, F. In *Reallexikon der Vorgeschichte,* vol. XI, edited by M. Ebert, s. v. "Schiff." Berlin: de Gruyter, 1927/28.

Bernabò-Brea, L., and Cavalier, M. *Il Castello di Lipari e il Museo Archeologico Eoliano.* Palermo: Flaccovio, 1979.

Besnier, M. *L'Ile Tiberine dans l'antiquité*. Paris: Bibliothèque des écoles françaises d' Athènes et de Rome, 1902.

Betts, J. In *Marine Archaeology*, edited by D. J. Blackman, pp. 325–38. Hamden: Archon, 1973.

Bianchi-Bandinelli, R. *Rome: The Late Empire*. New York: Braziller, 1971.

Bieber, M. *The Sculpture of the Hellenistic Age*. New York: Columbia University Press, 1955.

Blackman, D. J., ed. *Marine Archaeology*. Hamden: Archon, 1973.

Blegen, C. W. *Prosymna, the Helladic Settlement Preceding the Argive Heraeum*. Cambridge: Cambridge University Press, 1937.

Blinkenberg, C. *Asklepios og hans fraender i Hieron ved Epidauros*. Copenhagen, 1893.

———. "Triemiolia: Étude sur un type de navire rhodian." *Det. kgl Danske Videnskabernes Selskab. Archaeologisk-kunsthistorische Meddelelser* 2, no. 3 (1938): 3–59.

———. "Inscriptions." *Lindos*, vol. 2, part 1. Berlin: de Gruyter, 1941.

Boardman, J. *The Cretan Collection in Oxford*. Oxford: Clarendon Press, 1961.

———. "Ship Firedogs and Other Metalwork from Kavousi." *KrChron* 23 (1971): 5–8.

Boehlau, J., and Schefold, K. *Larisa am Hermos*. Vol. 3. *Die Kleinfunde*. Berlin: de Gruyter, 1941.

Bonino, M. "The Roman Transom Stern." *Mariner's Mirror* 49 (1963): 302–3.

———. "The Picene Ships of the 7th Century B.C. Engraved at Novilara (Pesaro, Italy)." *International Journal of Nautical Archaeology* 4 (1975): 11–20.

Boreux, C. "Études de nautique égyptienne." *MémInst* 50 (1924).

Bosanquet, R. C., and Dawkins, R. M. "The Unpublished Objects from the Palaikastro Excavations, 1904–1906." *BSA*, supplementary paper no. 1, 1923.

Bossert, H. T. *Altkreta*. Berlin: Wasmuth, 1923.

———. *Die altesten Kulturen des Mittelmeerkreises*. Vol. 2. *Alt-Anatolien*. Berlin: Wasmuth, 1942.

Breitenstein, N. *Catalogue of Terracottas*. Copenhagen: Munksgaard, 1941.

Brock, J. J. *Fortetsa. Early Greek Tombs near Knossos*. Cambridge: Cambridge University Press, 1957. *BSA*, supplementary paper no. 2.

Brøgger, A. W., and Shetelig, H. *The Viking Ships*. New York: Twayne, 1951; 2d. ed. 1971.

Broneer, O. "A Mycenaean Fountain on the Athenian Acropolis." *Hesperia* 8 (1939): 317–433.

———. "Excavations at Isthmia, Fourth Campaign, 1957–1958." *Hesperia* 28 (1959): 298–343.

Bruneau, P. "Isis Pélagia à Délos." *BCH* 85 (1961): 435–46.

———. "Isis Pélagia à Délos." *BCH* 87 (1963): 301–8.

———. "Les lampes." In *Explorations archéologiques de Délos*, vol. 26. Paris: École française d'Athènes/Boccard, 1965.

————. "Existe-t-il des statues d'Isis Pélagia?" *BCH* 98 (1974): 333–81.

Bruneau, P., and Ducat, J. *Guide de Délos*. Paris: École française d'Athènes, 1965.

Bruns, G. "Kuchwesen und Mahlzeiten." In *ArchHom*, vol. II. Göttingen: Vandenhoeck and Ruprecht, 1970.

Buchholz, H.-G. "Das Blei in der mykenische Kultur und in der bronze-zeitlichen Metallurgie Zyperns." *JdI* 87 (1972): 1–59.

Buchholz, H.-G., and Karageorghis, V. *Prehistoric Greece and Cyprus*. Tübingen, 1970.

Buchner, G. "Scavi e scoperti." *FA* 22 (1967): 131, no. 1949.

Buschor, E. "Ausgrabungen im Heraion von Samos 1936." *AA* 52 (1937): 203–22.

Caputo, G. "Il monumento di Cirene ella vittoria navale della battaglia d'Azio." *ParPass* 23 (1968): 230–33.

Cartault, A. "La trière athènienne." *Bibliothèque des écoles françaises d'Athènes et de Rome* 20 (1881): 11–70.

Caskey, J. L. "Excavations in Keos, 1960–1961." *Hesperia* 31 (1962): 263–83.

————. "Excavations in Ceos." *Deltion* 19 (1964a): 413–19.

————. "Excavations in Keos, 1963." *Hesperia* 33 (1964b): 314–35.

Casson, L. *The Ancient Mariners*. New York: Minerva, 1959.

————. "The Earliest Two-Masted Ship." *Archaeology* 16 (1963): 108–11.

————. *Illustrated History of Ships and Boats*. New York: Doubleday, 1964a.

————. "The Roman Blunt Prow." *Mariner's Mirror* 50 (1964b): 176.

————. *Ships and Seamanship in the Ancient World*. Princeton, N.J.: Princeton University Press, 1971.

————. "Bronze Age Ships. The Evidence of the Thera Wall Paintings." *International Journal of Nautical Archaeology* 4 (1975): 3–10.

Casson, S. *Techniques of Early Greek Sculpture*. Oxford: Clarendon Press, 1933.

Catling, H. W., ed. *JHS-AR*, 1979.

Cavvadias, P. *Fouilles d'Epidaure*. Athens: Vlastos, 1891.

Chadwick, J. *The Mycenaean World*. Cambridge: Cambridge University Press, 1976.

Champoiseau, A. "Le Victoire de Samothrace." *RA* 39 (1880): 11.

Charbonneaux, J.; Martin, R.; and Villard, F. *Archaic Greek Art*. New York: Braziller, 1971.

Chase, G. H. *Greek and Roman Antiquities: A Guide to the Classical Collection*. Boston: Museum of Fine Arts, 1950.

Chollot, M. "Étude de deux modèles de barques en terre cuite pêchées en mer." *Cahiers d'archéologie subaquatique* 4 (1975): 83–89.

Cohen, L. "Evidence for the Ram in the Minoan Period." *AJA* 42 (1938): 486–94.

Coldstream, J. N. *Greek Geometric Pottery*. London: Methuen, 1968.

Conticello, B., and Andreae, B. "Die Skulpturen von Sperlonga." *Antike Plastik* 14 (1974).

Couchoud, P. L., and Svoronos, J. "Le monument dit 'des taureaux' à Délos et le culte du navire sacré." *BCH* 45 (1921): 270–94.

Couilloud, M. T. "Les monuments funéraires de Rhénée." *Explorations archéologiques de Délos* 30 (1974).

Couilloud–Le Dinahet, M. T. "Recherches à Rhénée." *BCH* 102 (1978): 855–73.

Courbin, P. "Discoveries at Ancient Argos." *Archaeology* 9 (1956): 166–74.

———. "Une tombe géometrique d'Argos." *BCH* 81 (1957): 322–86.

Couve, L. "Notes ceramographiques." *BCH* 21 (1897): 444–74.

Daremberg, C. V.; Saglio, E.; and Pottier, E. *Dictionnaire des antiquités grecques et romaines*. Paris: Hachette, 1877–1919.

Davies, M. I. "Sailing, Rowing, and Sporting in One's Cups on the Wine-Dark Sea." In *Athens Comes of Age*. Princeton, N.J.: American Institute of Archaeology and Princeton University Press, 1978, pp. 72–95.

Dawkins, R. M. "Excavations at Palaikastro III." *BSA* 10 (1903–4): 192–226.

Decamps de Mertzenfeld, C. *Inventaire commenté des ivoires phéniciens et apparentés découverts dans le Proche-Orient*. Paris: de Boccard, 1954.

Defrasse, A., and Lechat, H. *Epidaure*. Paris: Librairies-Imprimeries réunies, 1895.

De Graeve, C. "Water Transport in Mesopotamia, 2000–579 BC." Ph.D. dissertation, Columbia University, 1978.

Deonna, W. "Les lampes antiques trouvées à Délos." *BCH* 32 (1908): 133–76.

———. "Le mobilier délien." *Explorations archéologiques de Délos* 18 (1938).

———. "Chenets à têtes animales, et chenets-navires. Le sens de leur décor." *Revue archéologique de l'Est et du centre Est* 10 (1959a): 24–37.

———. "Haches, broches et chenets dans une tombe géometrique d'Argos." *BCH* 83 (1959b): 247–53.

De Ridder, A. *Catalogue des bronzes trouvés sur l'Acropole d'Athènes*. Paris, 1896.

———. "L'ivoire en Crete et à Chypre." *Florilegium Melchior de Vogüé*, 1905, pp. 513–17.

Desborough, V. R. "Bird Vases." *KrChron* 24 (1972): 245–77.

Deubner, L. *Attische Feste*. Berlin: Keller, 1932.

Diamant, S. "A Short History of Archaeological Sieving at Francthi Cave, Greece." *JFA* 6 (1979): 203–17.

Diels, H. "Das Aphlaston der antiken Schiffe." *Zeitschrift des Vereins für Volkskunde* 25 (1915): 61–80.

Dikaios, P. *A Guide to the Cyprus Museum*. 3d. ed. Nicosia: Department of Antiquities, 1961.

Dodd, E. *Polynesian Seafaring*. New York: Dodd, Mead and Co., 1972.

Dohan, E. H. "Archaic Cretan Terracottas in America." *MMS* 3 (1930/31): 209–28.

Doumas, C. "Remarques sur la forme du bateau égéen à l'âge du bronze ancien." In *Valcomonica Symposium*. Paris, 1970/71, pp. 285–90.

Durrbach, F. *Inscriptions de Délos*, vols. I and II. Paris: Champion, 1926–29.

Durrbach, F., and Roussel, P. *Inscriptions de Délos,* vol. III. Paris: Champion, 1935.

Dussaud, R. *Les civilisations préhelléniques dans le bassin de la mer Égée.* 2d ed. Paris: Geunther, 1914.

Editors. "Ex-votos marins du Ponant." *Archeologia* 89 (1975): 76–77.

Edlund, I. E. M. "The Iron Age and Etruscan Vases in the Olcott Collection at Columbia University, New York." *TAPS* 70, no. 1 (1980).

Eiseman, C. J. "The Porticello Shipwreck. A Mediterranean Merchantman of 415–385 B.C." Ph.D. dissertation, University of Pennsylvania, 1979.

Eisman, M. M. "Attic Kyathos Painters." Ph.D. dissertation, University of Pennsylvania, 1971.

Ermeti, A. L. *L'Agora di Cirene*. Vol. 3, Part 1. *Il monumento navale*. Rome: "L'Erma" di Bretschneider, 1981.

Evans, A. J. "Recent Discoveries of Tarentine Terra Cottas." *JHS* 7 (1886): 1–50.

———. *The Prehistoric Tombs of Knossos.* London: Quaritch, 1906a.

———. "The Prehistoric Tombs of Knossos." *Archaeologia* 59, no. 2 (1906b): 391–562.

———. *The Palace of Minos at Knossos,* vols. I–IV. London: Macmillan, 1921–35.

Fairbanks, A. *Catalogue of the Greek and Etruscan Vases in the Museum of Fine Arts*, vol. I. Boston: Museum of Fine Arts, 1928.

Faure, P. "Nouvelles recherches sur trois sortes de sanctuaires crétois." *BCH* 91 (1967): 124–25.

Felbermeyer, J. "Sperlonga: The Ship of Odysseus." *Archaeology* 24 (1971): 136–45.

Fimmen, D. *Die kretisch-mykenische Kultur.* 2d ed. Leipzig and Berlin: Teubner, 1924.

Fittschen, K. *Untersuchungen zum Beginn der Sagendarstellungen bei den Griechen.* Berlin: Hessling, 1969.

Franzoni, L. *Bronzetti romani del Museo Archeologico di Verona.* Venice: Alfieri, 1973.

Fraser, P. M. "Archaeology in Greece, 1968–1969." *JHS-AR*, 1969, pp. 3–39.

Frickenhaus, A. "Der Schiffskarren des Dionysos in Athen." *JdI* 27 (1912): 61–79.

Froener, W. *Antiquités grecques*. Paris, 1878.

Frost, H. "The Ram from Marsala." *International Journal of Nautical Archaeology* 4, no. 2 (1975): 219–28.

Fuchs, S. *Kyrene*. Rome, 1942.

Fuchs, W. "Archäologische Forschungen und Funde in Sardinien 1949–
   1962." *AA* (1963): 323.

Gale, N. H., and Stos-Gale, Z. "Lead and Silver in the Ancient Aegean."
   Scientific American 244, no. 6 (1981): 176–92.

Gibbs, S. *Greek and Roman Sundials.* New Haven, Conn., and London: Yale
   University Press, 1976.

Gille, P. "Les navires à rames de l'antiquité, trières grecques et liburnes
   romaines." *JSav* 63 (1965): 36–72.

Goodchild, R. *Cyrene and Apollonia. An Historical Guide.* Tripoli: Department of Antiquities, 1963.

Göttlicher, A. *Materialien für ein Corpus der Schiffsmodelle im Altertum.* Mainz
   am Rhein: von Zabern, 1978.

———. "Römischen Lampen in Schiffsform." *Das Logbuch* 3, no. 15 (1979):
   97–100.

Göttlicher, A., and Werner, W. *Schiffsmodelle im alten Aegypten.* Wiesbaden:
   Arbeitskreis Histor. Schiffbau, 1971.

Graef, B., and Langlotz, E. *Die antiken Vasen von der Akropolis zu Athen,*
   vol. I. Berlin: de Gruyter, 1925.

Gray, D. "Seewesen." In *ArchHom,* vol. I, chapter G. Göttingen: Vandenhoeck and Ruprecht, 1974.

Green, M. J. "Romano-British Non-Ceramic Objects in South-east Britain." *ArchJ* 132 (1975): 54–70.

Greenhill, B. *Archaeology of the Boat.* Middletown, Conn.: Wesleyan University Press, 1976.

Grinsell, L. V. "The Boat of the Dead in the Bronze Age." *Antiquity* 15
   (1941): 360–70.

Gusmani, R. *Lydisches Wörterbuch.* Heidelberg: Carl Winter, 1964.

Gwyn Griffiths, J., ed. *Apuleius of Madauros: The Isis-Book (Metamorphoses,
   Book XI).* Leiden: Brill, 1975.

Haddon, A. C., and Hornell, J. *Canoes of Oceania,* vols. I–II. Honolulu:
   B. P. Bishop Museum, 1936–37.

Hall, H. R. *The Civilization of Greece in the Bronze Age.* London: Methuen,
   1928.

Hansen, H. J. *Schiffsmodelle. Die Geschichte der Schiffbaukunst im Spiegel zeit-
   genössischer Modelle.* Hamburg: Oldenburg, 1972.

Harris, J. "Le Geay, Piranesi, and International Neo-Classicism in Rome,
   1740–1750." In *Essays in the History of Architecture . . . for R. Wittkoer,*
   edited by D. Fraser. London: Phaidon, 1967.

———. *Sir William Chambers.* London: Zwemmer, 1970.

Haspels, C. H. E. *Attic Black-Figured Lekythoi.* Paris: de Boccard,
   1936.

Hautecoeur, L. *Histoire de l'architecture classique en France,* vol. VI. Paris:
   Picard, 1955.

Helbig, W. *Führer durch die öffentlichen Sammlungen klassischer Alterthümer in
   Rom.* 4th ed. Tübingen, 1966.

Herbig, R. "Philister und Dorier." *JdI* 55 (1940): 58–89.

Higgins, R. A. *Catalogue of the Terracottas in the . . . British Museum,* vols.
    I–II. London: British Museum, 1954.
Homolle, T. "Comptes des hiéropes du Temple d'Apollon délien." *BCH*
    6 (1882): 1–167.
————. "Inventaires des temples déliens en l'année 364." *BCH* 10 (1886):
    461–75.
————. "Comptes et inventaires des temples déliens en l'année 279." *BCH*
    14 (1890): 389–511.
————. "Inscriptions de Délos." *BCH* 27 (1903): 62–103.
Hood, S. *The Minoans.* London: Thames and Hudson, 1971.
Hornell, J. "The Origins and Ethnological Significance of Indian Boat De-
    sign." *Memoirs of the Asiatic Society of Bengal* 7, no. 3 (1920): 139–256.
————. "The Baganda Canoe: The Problems of Its Origin." *Mariner's Mirror*
    19 (1933): 439–45.
————. "The Prow of the Ship: Sanctuary of the Tutelary Deity." *Man* 43
    (1943): 121–28.
————. *Water Transport.* Cambridge: Cambridge University Press, 1946.
Howland, R. H. *Greek Lamps and Their Survivals.* Athenian Agora, vol.
    IV. Princeton, N.J.: American School of Classical Studies, 1958.
Humphreys, S. C. Review of *Emergence of Civilization,* by C. Renfrew.
    International Journal of Nautical Archaeology 2, no. 1 (1973): 219.
————. "Artists' Mistakes." *International Journal of Nautical Archaeology* 7,
    no. 1 (1978): 78–79.
Hutchinson, R. W. *Prehistoric Crete.* Harmondsworth: Penguin, 1962.
Iakovides, S. *Perati,* vols. 2–3. Athens: Hetaires, 1969.
Jacobsen, T. W. "17,000 Years of Greek Prehistory." *Scientific American*
    234, no. 6 (1976): 76–87.
Jacopi, G. *L'antro di Tiberio a Sperlonga.* Rome, 1966.
Jeffery, L. H. *The Local Scripts of Archaic Greece.* Oxford: Clarendon Press,
    1961.
Jenkins, G. K. *Ancient Greek Coins.* New York: Putnam, 1972.
Johnston, P. F. Review of *Göttlicher,* 1978. *American Institute of Nautical
    Archaeology Newsletter* 5, no. 4 (Winter 1979): 6–7.
Johnston, P. F.; Sands, J. O.; and Steffy, J. R. "The Cornwallis Cave
    Shipwreck, Yorktown, Virginia." *International Journal of Nautical Ar-
    chaeology* 7, no. 3 (1978): 205–26.
Johnstone, P. "Stern First in the Stone Age." *International Journal of Nautical
    Archaeology* 2 (1973): 3–11.
Jones, H. S. *Catalogue of Ancient Sculptures Preserved in the Muncipal Collections
    of Rome: The Sculptures of the Museo Capitolino.* Oxford: Clarendon
    Press, 1912.
Jordan, B. *The Athenian Navy in the Classical Period.* Berkeley: University
    of California, 1975.
Karageorghis, V. "Myth and Epic in Mycenaean Vase Painting." *AJA* 62
    (1958): 383–87.
————. "Ten Years of Archaeology in Cyprus, 1953–1962." *AA* 78 (1963a):
    551.

―――. "Une tombe de guerrier à Palaepaphos." *BCH* 87 (1963b): 265–300.

―――. *Salamis in Cyprus.* London: Thames and Hudson, 1969.

―――. *Report of the Cyprus Department of Antiquities 1972.* Nicosia: Department of Antiquities, 1972.

Karo, G. "Orient und Hellas in archaischer Zeit." *AthMitt* 45 (1920): 106–56.

Katzev, M. L. "A Replica of the Kyrenia Ship." *Institute of Nautical Archaeology Newsletter* 7, no. 1 (Spring 1980): 1–6.

Kaufmann, C. M. *Ägyptische Terrakotten der griechischen-römischen und koptischen Epoche aus der Faijum und andren Fundstatten.* Leipzig and Cairo, 1913.

Kennedy, D. H. "Cable Reinforcement of the Athenian Trireme." *Mariner's Mirror* 62 (1976): 159–68.

Kern, O. *Inscriptiones Graecae.* Bonn: Marcus and Weber, 1913.

Kilinski, K. "Boeotian Dancers Group." *AJA* 82 (1978): 173–91.

Kirk, G. S. "Ships on Geometric Vases." *BSA* 44 (1949): 93–153.

―――. "The Ship-Rhyton in Boston." *AJA* 55 (1951): 339–43.

Kopcke, G. "Neue Holzfunde aus dem Heraion von Samos." *AthMitt* 82 (1967): 100–148.

Köster, A. *Das antike Seewesen.* Berlin: Schatz and Parrhysius, 1923.

Krauss, F. "Die Prora an der Tiberinsel in Rom." *RömMitt* 59 (1944): 159–72.

Kunze, E. *Kretische Bronzereliefs.* Stuttgart: Kohlhammer, 1931.

Kurtz, D. C., and Boardman, J. *Greek Burial Customs.* Ithaca, N.Y.: Cornell University Press, 1971.

Kyrieleis, H. "Archaische Holzfunde aus Samos." *AthMitt* 95 (1980): 87–147.

Landström, B. *Das Schiff.* Gütersloh, 1961.

―――. *Ships of the Pharaohs.* New York: Doubleday, 1970.

Laurinsich, A. *CVA Bologna,* vol. 2. Milan: Casa Editrice d'Arte Bestetti e Tumminelli, n.d.

Lauter, H. "Zur Datierung der Skulpturen von Sperlonga." *RömMitt* 76 (1969): 162–73.

Laviosa, C. "La marina micenea." *ASAtene* 47–48 (1969–70): 7–40.

Le Gall, J. "Les bas-reliefs de la statue du 'Tibre' au Louvre." *RA* 22 (1944): 38–55.

―――. "Un 'modèle réduit' de navire marchand romain." In *Melanges Charles Picard.* Paris: Presses Universitaires de France, 1949, pp. 607–17.

―――. *Recherches sur le culte du Tibre.* Paris: Publications de l'Institut d'Art et Archéologie de l'Université de Paris, 1953.

Lehmann, K. *Samothrace: A Guide.* New York: New York University Press, 1955.

Lehmann, K., and Lehmann, P. W. *Samothracian Reflections.* Princeton, N.J.: Princeton University Press, 1973.

Lenzen, H. J. "XXI Warke-Kampagne." *AA* 78 (1963/64): 642.

Lewis, N. *Samothrace,* vol. I. New York: Pantheon, 1958.

Lilliu, G. "Small Nuraghian Bronzes from Sardinia." *Antiquity and Survival* 1 (1955): 268–90.

——. *Sculture della Sardegna Nuragica.* 2d ed. Cagliari: Zattera, 1966.

Lindquist, S. "The Boat Models from Roos Carr." *ActaA* 13 (1942): 235–42.

Littman, E. *Lydian Inscriptions.* Sardis, vol. 6, no. 1. Leiden: Brill, 1916.

Lloyd, A. B. "Were Necho's Triremes Phoenician?" *JHS* 95 (1975): 45–61.

Long, C. R. "The Ayia Triadha Sarcophagus: A Study of Late Minoan and Mycenaean Funerary Practices and Beliefs." *SIMA* 41 (1974).

L'Orange, H. P. "Sperlonga Again. Supplementary Remarks on the 'Scylla' and the 'Ship.' " *ActaIRN* 4 (1969): 25–26.

Loud, G. "The Megiddo Ivories." *OIP* 52 (1939).

——. "Megiddo II." *OIP* 62 (1948).

Lowrie, W. "A Jonah Monument in the New York Metropolitan Museum." *AJA* 5 (1901): 51–57.

Macalister, R. A. S. *The Excavation of Gezer 1902–1905 and 1907–1909,* vol. II. London: J. Murray, 1912.

McGrail, S., ed. *Sources and Techniques in Boat Archaeology.* BAR Supplementary Series 29, Archaeological Series No. 1. Greenwich: National Maritime Museum, 1977.

MacIver, D. R. *Villanovans and Early Etruscans.* Oxford: Clarendon Press, 1924.

Maraghiannis, G. *Antiquités Crétoises,* vol. I. Vienna: Angerer, 1911–1915.

Marcadé, J. "Sur une base lindienne en forme de proue." *RA* 26 (1946): 147–52.

Marinatos, S. "La marine créto-mycenienne." *BCH* 57 (1933): 170–235.

——. *Excavations at Thera VI.* Athens: Hetaireia, 1974.

Marinatos, S., and Hirmer, M. *Kreta und das mykenische Hellas.* Munich: Hirmer, 1959.

——. *Kreta, Thera und das mykenische Hellas.* 3d ed. Munich: Hirmer, 1976.

Marsden, P. "A Roman Transom Stern." *Mariner's Mirror* 49 (1963): 143–44.

Marstrander, S. "Building a Hide Boat. An Archaeological Experiment." *International Journal of Nautical Archaeology* 5, no. 1 (1976): 13–22.

Martin, R. *L'Agora.* Études Thasiennes. Paris: École française d'Athènes, 1959.

Marucchi, O. "Benevento." *NSc* 5, no. 1 (1904): 107–27.

Mau, A. "Rostra Caesaris." *RömMitt* 20 (1905): 230–66.

Meyer, M. "Altpulische Terrakotten." *JdI* 25 (1910): 176:92.

Meiggs, R. "The Dating of Fifth-Century Attic Inscriptions." *JHS* 86 (1966): 86–98.

Merker, G. S. "The Hellenistic Sculpture of Rhodes." *SIMA* 40 (1973): 3–34.

Michaud, J.-P. "Chronique des Fouilles en 1973." *BCH* 98 (1974): 579–722.

Mitten, D. G., and Doeringer, S. F. *Master Bronzes from the Classical World.* Mainz: Fogg Art Museum, 1967.

Moll, F. *Das Schiff in der bildenden Kunst.* Bonn: Shroeder, 1929.

Montelius, O. *La civilisation primitive en Italie depuis l'introduction des métaux.* Stockholm, 1904.

———. *La Grèce préclassique.* Stockholm: Haggströms, 1924.

Moretti, G., and Caprino, C. *Il Museo delle Navi roman di Nemi.* Rome: Instituto Poligrafico dello stato, 1957.

Moretti, M. *La Tomba della Nave.* Milan: Lerici, 1961.

Morgan, C. H., Jr., "The Terracotta Figurines from the North Slope of the Acropolis." *Hesperia* 4 (1935): 193–97.

Morrison, J. S. "The Greek Trireme." *Mariner's Mirror* 27 (1941): 14–44.

———. "Hemiolia, Trihemiolia." *International Journal of Nautical Archaeology* 9, no. 2 (1980): 121–26.

Morrison, J. S., and Williams, R. T. *Greek Oared Ships 900–322 B.C.* Cambridge: Cambridge University Press, 1968.

Mosso, A. *The Dawn of Mediterranean Civilisation.* New York: Baker and Taylor, n.d.

Muller, H. W. *Il Culto di Iside nell'antica Benevento.* Benevento: Museo del Sannio, 1971.

Mylonas, G. E. *Mycenae in the Mycenaean Age.* Princeton, N.J.: Princeton University Press, 1966.

Nauert, J. P. "The Hagia Triada Sarcophagus: An Iconographical Study." *AntK* 8 (1965): 91–98.

Newhall, A. "The Corinthian Kerameikos." *AJA* 35 (1931): 1–30.

Nilsson, M. P. *The Minoan-Mycenaean Religion and Its Survival in Greek Religion.* 2d ed. Lund: Gleerup, 1950.

Ochsenschlager, E. "Mud Objects from al-Hiba." *Archaeology* 27 (1974): 162–74.

Ohly, D. "Holz." *AthMitt* 68 (1953): 77–126.

Orlandini, P. "Tipologia e cronologia del materiale archeologico di Gela dalla nuova fondacione di Timoleonte all'età di Ierone II." *ArchCl* 9 (1957): 153–73.

Orlandos, A. K. "Zakro." *To Ergon,* 1970–71, pp. 167–85.

Orsi, P. "Scavi e trovamenti . . . ." *Museo italiano di Antichita Classica* 2 (1888): 729–30.

Paglieri, S. "Origine e diffusione delle navi etrusco-italiche." *StEtr* 28 (1960): 209–31.

Papadopoulou-Zapheiropoulou, P. "Xronika: Melos." *Deltion* 21 (1966): 386–87.

Paribeni, R. "Necropoli del territorio Copenate." *MonAnt* 16 (1906): 277–490.

———. "Il sarcofago dipinto di Hagia Triada." *MonAnt* 19 (1908): 6–86.

Paton, J. M., ed. *The Erechtheum.* Cambridge, Mass.: Harvard University Press, 1927.

Pauly, A. F. von, and Wissowa, G. *Paulys RealEncyclopädie der klassischen Altertumswissenschaft.* Stuttgart: Metzler, 1893–1963.

Pausanius. *Guide to Greece.* Translated by P. Levi. Harmondsworth: Penguin, 1979.

Payne, H., et al. *Perachora: The Sanctuaries of Hera Akraia and Limenia,* vol. I. Oxford: Clarendon Press, 1940.

Pendlebury, J. D. S. *The Archaeology of Crete.* London: Methuen, 1939.

Perdrizet, P. *Les terre cuites grecques d'Égypte de la collection Fouquet.* Paris: Berger-Levrault, 1921.

Perlsweig, J. *Lamps from the Athenian Agora.* Princeton, N.J.: American School of Classical Studies, 1963.

Pernice, E. "Erwerbungen der Antikensammlungen in Deutschland: Berlin Antiquarium." *AA* 19 (1904): 29.

Perrot, G., and Chipiez, C. *Histoire de l'art dans l'antiquité.* Paris: Hachette, 1882–1914.

Petersen, E. "Comitium und Rostra." *RömMitt* 21 (1906): 193–210.

Petrakos, V. "Meletai." *Deltion* 29 (1974): 98–99.

Petrie, W. M. F. *Naqada and Ballas 1895.* London: Quaritch, 1896.

Petronius Arbiter, Titus. Translated by M. Heseltine. *Satyricon* London and Cambridge, Mass.: Heinemann and Harvard University Press, 1956.

Pfuhl, E. *Malerei und Zeichnung der Griechen.* Munich: F. Bruckmann, 1923.

Picard, G.-C. *Les Trophées romains. Contributions à l'histoire de la religion et de l'art triomphal de Rome.* Paris: Bibliothèque des écoles françaises d'Athènes et de Rome, 1957.

Piggott, S. *Ancient Europe.* Chicago: Aldine, 1965.

Pinza, G. "Monumenti primitivi della Sardegna." *MonAnt* 11 (1901): 5–280.

Pittakes, K. S. "To en to Erechtheio eurethen ploion." *ArchEph,* 1862, pp. 91–94.

Plaoutine, N. *CVA.* Vol. 15. *France.* Part 1. *Paris Petit Palais.* Paris: 1941.

Plassert, A. "Fouilles de Délos." *BCH* 36 (1912): 387–435.

Price, T. H. *Kourotrophos: Cults and Representations of the Greek Nursing Deities.* Leiden: Brill, 1978.

Procopius. *History of the Wars.* Translated by H. B. Dewing. London and New York: Heinemann and Putnam, 1928.

Qualls, C. "Boats of Mesopotamia before 2000 B.C." Ph.D. dissertation, Columbia University, 1980.

Randall-MacIver, D. *Villanovans and Early Etruscans.* Oxford: Clarendon Press, 1924.

Reinach, A. J. "Le Sarcophage de Haghia Triada." *RA* 12 (1908): 278–88.

———. "Cockerell à Délos." *RA* 4, no. 19 (1912): 260–312.

Reinhardt, K. "Geschichte des Schiffbau an Modellen sichtbar gemacht." *Beiträge zur Geschichte der Technik und Industrie* 29 (1940): 44–52.

Reisner, G. A. *Models of Ships and Boats.* Cairo: Imprimerie de l'institut français d'archéologie orientale, 1913.

Renfrew, C. "Cycladic Metallurgy and the Aegean Early Bronze Age." *AJA* 71 (1967): 1–20.

————. *The Emergence of Civilisation; the Cyclades and the Aegean in the Third Millenium B.C.* London: Methuen, 1972.

Rhousopoulos, A. S. "Poikila." *ArchEph*, 1862, pp. 35–39.

Richter, C. "Die römische Rednerbühre." *JDAI* 4 (1889): 1–18.

Richter, G. M. A. "Sperlonga." *Princeton Encylopedia of Classical Sites,* edited by R. Stillwell. Princeton, N.J.: Princeton University Press, 1976, p. 856.

Robinson, E. *Annual Report of the Boston Museum of Fine Arts* 24 (1899): 56–57.

Rodgers, W. L. *Greek and Roman Naval Warfare.* Annapolis: Naval Institute Press, 1937.

Rolley, C. "Bronzes et bronziers des âges obscurs (XIIe–VIIe siècles av. J.C.)." *RA*, 1975, pp. 155–60.

Rossiter, S. *Rome and Environs.* London: Benn, 1971.

Rubin de Cervin, G. "The Roman galley of the Tiberine Island." *Mariner's Mirror* 40 (1954): 309–11.

Rudolph, R. C. "Boat Models from Early Chinese Tombs." *AJA* 78 (1974): 65–68.

Rupp, D. W. "Catalogue of Ship Representations in Roman Mosaics and Monumental Painting." M.A. thesis. University of Pennsylvania, n.d.

Säflund, G. *Fynden i Tiberius grotten.* Stockholm, 1966.

————. "The Polyphemus and Scylla Groups at Sperlonga." *Stockholm Studies in Classical Archaeology* 9 (1972).

Sakellarakis, I. A. "Elephantinon ploion ek Mukenon." *ArchEph*, 1971, pp. 188–233.

Sakellarakis, I. A., and Sapouna-Sakellarakis, E. "Drama of Death in a Minoan Temple." *National Geographic* 159, no. 2 (1981): 204–23.

Sams, G. K. "Beer in the City of Midas." *Archaeology* 30, no. 2 (1977): 108–15.

Schachermeyr, F. *Die minoische Kultur des alten Kreta.* Stuttgart: Kohlhammer, 1964.

————. *Agäis und Orient.* Vienna: Böhlaus, 1967.

Schaeffer, C. F. A. *Missions en Chypre 1932–1936.* Paris: Geuthner, 1936.

Scheel, W. "Die Rostra am Westende des Forum Romanum." *RömMitt* 43 (1928): 176–255.

Seager, R. B. "Excavations on the Island of Mochlos, Crete, in 1908." *AJA* 13 (1909): 273–303.

————. *Explorations on the Island of Mochlos.* Boston and New York: American School of Classical Studies, 1912.

Seyrig, H. "Antiquités de Beth-Maré." *Syria* 28 (1951): 101–23.

Sichtermann, H. "Das veröffentliche Sperlonga." *Gymnasium,* 1966, pp. 220–39.

Sleeswyk, A. W. "The prow of the 'Nike of Samothrace' Reconsidered." *International Journal of Nautical Archaeology* 11, no. 3 (1982): 233–43.

Smith, C. H. *Catalogue of the Forman Collection.* London: Sotheby, June 1899.

————. "Excavations in Melos, 1897." *BSA* 3 (1896–97): 1–30.

Smith, W., ed. *A Dictionary of Greek and Roman Biography and Mythology*. London: John Murray, 1880.

Snodgrass, A. M. *The Dark Age of Greece*. Edinburgh: Edinburgh University Press, 1971.

Stais, V. *Marbres et bronzes du Musée National*. Athens: Sakellarios, 1907.

Stillwell, A. N. *The Potters' Quarter. The Terracottas*. Corinth, vol. XV, part II. Princeton, N.J.: American School of Classical Studies, 1952.

Stillwell, R., ed. *Princeton Encyclopedia of Classical Sites*. Princeton, N.J.: Princeton University Press, 1976.

Stucchi, S. *L'Agora di Cirene*. Rome, 1959.

———. *Cirene 1957–1966*. Tripoli, 1967.

Tamvaki, A. "Some Unusual Mycenaean Terracottas from the Citadel House Area, 1954–1969." *BSA* 68 (1973): 207–65.

Tarn, W. W. "The Greek Warship." *JHS* 25 (1905): 137–56, 204–24.

———. "The Dedicated Ship of Antigonus Gonatas." *JHS* 30 (1910): 209–22.

Taylor, J. du Plat, ed. *Marine Archaeology*. New York: Crowell, 1966.

Thiersch, H. "Die Nike von Samothrace, ein Rhodisches Werk und Anathem." *Nachrichten von der Akad. des Wissenschaften in Göttingen*, 1931, pp. 337–56.

Thurneyssen, J. "Artists' Mistakes. A Reply." *International Journal of Nautical Archaeology* 8, no. 3 (1979): 254.

Tilley, A. F. "L'énigme de la Trireme." *Archaeologia* 37 (1970): 60–61.

Torr, C. *Ancient Ships*, 2d ed. Chicago: Argonaut, 1964.

Touchais, G. "Chronique des fouilles en 1977." *BCH* 102 (1978): 655–56.

Trendall, A. D. "Archaeology in South Italy and Sicily." *JHS-AR*, 1966–67.

Tsountas, M. "Kykladika III." *ArchEph*, 1899, pp. 90–91.

Tufnell, O.; Inge, C. H.; and Harding, L. *Lachish II: The Fosse Temple*. Oxford: Oxford University Press, 1940.

Tyree, E. L. "Cretan Sacred Caves: Archaeological Evidence." Ph.D. dissertation, University of Missouri, 1974.

Ure, P. N. *Boeotian Pottery of the Geometric and Archaic Style*. Paris, 1927.

———. " 'Kothons' and Kufas." *ArchEph*, 1937, pp. 258–62.

Vallois, R. *L'Architecture hellenique et hellenistique à Délos*. Paris: de Boccard, 1944.

Van Deeman, E. B. "The So-called Flavian Rostra." *AJA* 13 (1909): 170–86.

Van Effenterre, H., and Van Effenterre, M. *Mallia. Centre Politique*. Vol. 1. *L'Agora*. Paris: École française d'Athènes, 1969.

Vermeule, C. *Greek, Etruscan and Roman Art. The Classical Collection of the Museum of Fine Arts*. Boston: Museum of Fine Arts, 1963.

Vermeule, E. *Greece in the Bronze Age*. Chicago: University of Chicago Press, 1972.

Von Bissing, F. W. "Die sardinischen Bronzen." *RömMitt* 43 (1928): 19–89.

von Blanckenhagen, P. H. Review of Conticello and Andreae, 1974. *AJA* 80 (1976): 99–104.

von Gerkan, A. "Der Nordmarkt und der Hafen an der Löwenbucht." *Milet*, vol. I, no. 6. Berlin and Leipzig: de Gruyter, 1922.

Von Schneider, R. "Neuere Erwerbungen der Antikensammlung des Österreichische Kaiserhauses in Wien 1880–1891." *AA* 7 (1892): 116.

Wachsmann, S. "The Ships of the Sea Peoples (*IJNA* 10.3: 187–220): Additional Notes." *International Journal of Nautical Archaeology* 11, no. 4. (1982): 297–304.

Waiblinger, A. *CVA*. Vol. 17. *Louvre*. Paris: de Boccard, 1974.

Walter-Karydi, E. "Die Entstehung der griechischen Statuenbasis." *AntK* 23, no. 1 (1980): 3–12.

Walters, H. B. *Catalogue of the Terracottas . . . in the British Museum*. London: British Museum, 1903.

———. *History of Ancient Pottery,* vols. I–II. London: John Murray, 1905.

———. *Catalogue of the Greek and Etruscan Vases in the British Museum*, vol. I, part II. London: Trustees of the British Museum, 1912.

———. *Catalogue of the Greek and Roman Lamps in the British Museum*. London: Trustees of the British Museum, 1914.

Watzinger, C. *Griechischen Vasen in Tübingen*. Reutlingen: Gryphius, 1924.

Weber, W. *Die ägyptisch-griechischen Terrakotten,* vol. II. Berlin: Curtius, 1914.

Weicker, G. *Der Seelenvogel in der alten Litteratur und Kunst*. Leipzig, 1902.

Werner, W. "Nautische Denkmäler im Altertum." *Das Logbuch* 6, no. 2 (1970): 12–18; no. 3 (1975): 94–101.

Westerberg, K. "Cypriote Ships from the Bronze Age to c. 500 B.C." *SIMA Pocket-Books* 22 (1983).

Whibley, L. *A Companion to Greek Studies*. 4th ed. Cambridge: Cambridge University Press, 1931.

Wilamowitz-Moellendorff, U. von. "Lesefruchte." *Hermes* 54 (1919): 46–74.

Woelcke, K. "Beiträge zur Geschichte des Tropaion." *Bonner Jahrbücher* 120 (1911): 127–235.

Wooley, L. *Ur Excavations: The Royal Cemetery,* vol. II. Oxford: British Museum and University of Pennsylvania, 1934.

———. "New Clues to Hittite History in Syria." *ILN*, 9 October 1937, pp. 604–6.

———. "Gaps Filled in Syrian History of 3520 Years Ago." *ILN*, 17 September 1938, pp. 503–5

Xanthoudides, S. *The Vaulted Tombs of Mesara*. London: Hodder and Stoughton, 1924.

Zervos, C. *L'art de la Crète néolithique et minoenne*. Paris: Éditions 'Cahiers d'art,' 1956.

———. *L'art des Cyclades du début à la fin de l'âge du bronze, 2500–1100 avant notre ère*. Paris: Éditions 'Cahiers d'art,' 1957.

Zimmerman, J.-L. In *Art antique. Collections privées de Suisse Romande,* by J. Dörig. Genf: Éditions archéologiques de l'Université de Genève, 1975.

Index

Transom, 37, 153n*18*
Traostalos (Crete), 23
Trierarch, 160n*55*
Trieres, 46, 76–77, 83, 88, 90–91, 120–22, 133–37
Trihemiolia, 90–91, 93, 102, 159n*41*
Trireme, 161n*81*
Triton, 49, 68
Troy, 134
Tynnichos, 134
Tyre, 136
Tyrrhenians. *See* Etruscans

Ur, 11, 150nn*42,61*

Vase painting, 1, 45, 48–49, 67

Victory (Nike), 88, 93–95, 102, 137, 158n*37*, 159n*51*, 160n*70*, 161n*83*
Villanovan Iron Age, 145
Virgil: *Aeneid,* 161n*77*
Vulci, 96

Wall painting, 1, 16–17, 47, 85
Warka (Mesopotamia), 135
Wood (wooden), 46–47, 50, 54–64, 126
Written sources, 75. *See also* Epigraphy; Inscription

Zakros (Crete), 24
Zankle, 78, 157n*26*
Zeus Kasios, 135